HAUNTS OF WILD

OR-

Poems of Woods, Wilds and Waters,

By

ISAAC McLELLAN,

FISHES AND FISHING.

ANGLING.

When the rosy flame of day crimsons the silvery
    mist.
And from the valley rolls away the haze by sunbeams kiss'd,
Then to the the bowery woods I pass with angling rod and line,
While yet the dewdrops on the grass, like lucid diamonds shine.
How vast the mossy forest halls, how silent, full of gloom !
Thro' the arch'd roof the daybeam falls. like torchlight in a tomb.
Brown trunks of trees rise all around, like pillars in a church of old,
And the wind fills them with a sound as if a bell were tolled.
Where falls the sparkling stream in bubbles clear and bright,
Along whose grassy margin gleam flowers lovely to the sight,
There silently I stand, watching my trout-flies play.
And eagerly draw to the brink my speckled prey. Oft ere the carrion-bird hath
left its eyrie, the dead tree,
Or ere the eagle's wing hath cleft the cloud in heaven's blue sea.
Or ere the lark's swift pinion speeds to meet the early day,
My foot hath press'd the yellow reeds, my rod sought out its prey.
And when the twilight, with a blush on her fair cheek. slips by,
And evening's universal hush fills all the darkening sky,
And steadily the tapers burn in distant village homes,
Then from the peaceful stream I turn, and from the forest glooms.

THE ANGLER.

I sing the angler's joys the angler's toil, That lure him from the pent-up city's din. From luxury and pride and greed of gain, From strife of riches and resorts of sin.

They lead him forth to Nature's purest scenes Where he can contemplate in placid mood ; Can look from Nature " up to nature's God," Roaming by tranquil stream and drooping wood.

How pure, refined, these true delights must be,

To those who love to view each wondrous scene, Can with instructed eye these worlds behold, The solemn groves, the fields of living green,

How pitiful, how trivial must appear,

The scenes they left, the crowd, the noisy mart. As Nature's kindly spell refines the mind, And soothes, and purifies the human heart.

'Mid the sublimities that rock and mount, Forest and torrent everywhere combine, The mind is toned harmonious with the scene, The knee is lowly bent at Nature's shrine.

As the grand shadows sweep the mountain brow, As the brisk breeze sweeps thro' the woodlands
deep,

The soul is touched, the senses full receive The grandeur and the music as they sweep. 'Mid the repose of Nature's gentle realms,

Where hills uprise from grassy meadows bright. Where village-spire peeps o'er the tufted trees. And chiming bells to evening prayer invite.

Where clank of distant mill-wheel in the air, Is scarcely heard above each rural sound, The hum of bee, the song of tuneful bird, The low of cattle in the pastures round.

When images of peace possess the soul, . The angler's mind assumes a musing train Banish'd are sordid struggles of the world, The traffic and the fraud. the lust of gain.

The soul with purer influence is stirr'd,

The inmost thoughts are of a gentler mood, Fill'd with more charity for human sin, Thrill'd with more genial impulses of good. Dear Angler! as you lay your tackle by Shut the slim rod and fold the silken line. Think, as the months inclement, bluster past, Of summer pleasures and of worlds divine.

THE ANGLER'S REALM.

The angler finds in all this ample realm Pleasures, allurements wheresoe're he roams. By Mississippi floods, Ohio's streams. By Alleghany mounts or river foams, By solemn woods or in the vallies green, In rocky gulch. where endless torrents pour, In gorge and ravines, where steep waterfalls Incessant beat the borders of the shore. By every stream in Nature's broad domain. In placid lake, clear brook and spacious bay.

In Northern tides where salmon plunge and leap He finds rich pastimes, a glad holiday. He reaps a harvest for his rod and line In Adirondack lakes. so crystal-clear, In placid ponds and rivulets of Maine. He seeks enjoyment to his heart so dear. Gains health and transport on each watery plain From far Pacific to Atlantic main.

In lovliest scenes he rare allurments finds.
Where winds the rippling brook thro' meadows green,
Casting the feathered fly, the barbed hook O'er boiling rapids or in depths serene.
So ever in such sport he seeks delight.
By shadowy grove and in the currents pure, For charms of Nature everywhere prevail, In gloom of forest or on sylvan moor.
He finds a beauty, an eternal charm
In all the haunts beneath the arching skies,
In summer greenery, in autumn flush,
In groves frost-colored by commingled dyes,
In spring-tide brooks. bright-edged with varied flowers.
Fring'd with red roses and the lilies white, He gains enticements for his every sense, A transport and perfume, a fresh delight ;
He communes with kind Nature in her homes. Charm'd with new raptures wheresoe'er he roams. Nature's fair features ever smile the same. For lapse of years may ne'er disturb her face. She welcomes the good angler to her shrine, And bounteous greets him in each sylvan place. Each stream he haunts is rich with spangled trout. In estuaries wide. in channels steep;
He takes the salmon or the tarpon-king.
And bass and blue-fish by the watery deep.

THE ANGLER'S HAUNT.

Soon as the earliest shaft of light
Shoots o'er the summit of the wood, Touching with gold each tufted height.
Tinging the ripples of the flood, The angler stands on river banks
Where fall the willow's drooping plumes. Where grow the osiers green and rank
And water-lilies ope their blooms.
He loves the walk o'er the grassy plain,
The tramp thro' tussock and thick swale. The path through the uplands' high domain.
Or adown the hollow vale.
There in some sweet, secluded place
He scans the water's dimpled sweep, Notes where the rippling eddies race,
And where the trout schools leap,
Then swings his rod with sturdy hand.
Casts the long line with skill.
And quick is bent the tapering wand And the reel singeth shrill.
Mayhap he seeks the pebbled shore
Where billows curl their crest.
Or round the weedy boulders pour. Forever frothing. ne'er at rest ;
And there upon some jutting rock
He swings the rod. he casts the line.
He drags the bluefish from the brine.

THE ANGLER'S JOURNAL.

As the gay songsters in the budding grove Welcome with melodies so liquid sweet,
The roseate Spring-time in each orchard spaceChant:ng glad poems in each wood-retreatSo doth the angler with blithe greetings hail The May days' dancing over hill and dale. Bearing fresh garlands of the rose and pink, Wreaths of the crocus and the lilies pale. So doth his soul o'erflow with perfect joy, Seeing the streamlets break their icy chain And run rejoicing down the grassy slopes. Leaping with laughter o'er the meadow plain. So the keen anglers welcome with a cheer, This new-born journal. *sacred to their art. Whose printed page shall celebrate the bliss,

That in sweet Spring-time thrills the angler's heart. In its fair lines the early birds shall sing. Transcendent flowers enamel all the mead. 'Twill echo the soft merriment of brooks, And to fresh streams most ardent anglers lead.

Musing o'er th' Angler's Journal, he will trace, In fancy the clear stream he knew of old.

The brook that crept adown the meadow-space, Slipping in ripples o'er the sands of gold : Again, as in old times, he'll cast the line, The humble worm or artificial fly,

Where the slow stream in purple deeps would sleep Or sparkle o'er the pebbles merrily. In thought he will revisit the old pond. That spreads its placid surface by the mill. Its shores with lily-pads, and willows lin'd,

Where the *gay* song-birds pour'd incessant trill. He will remember and explore again.

Those noble streams in Adirondack woods ; Homes of the black-bass, and the speckled trout, That love the shades of forest solitudes.

Again will breathe the spicy woodland air,

The fir-tree's breath, the pine-woods rare perfume ; Will build with leafy boughs his forest camp, Free and delighted with the sunless gloom.

In this fair Journal he will find record,

Of anglers' joys in pathless woods of Maine. At the head waters of Penobscot stream,

Or where dear Greenwood spreads its watery plain. Here. too, he'll share exilerating joys,

Reading of triumphs by the billowy shore,

At Long Branch, Sheepshead or Canarsie bays, Or where the surf by green Long Island pours. Fairest of all, the angler's paradise

Florida, worthy of supremest fame

Where channel-bass and sheepshead cleave the deeps,

And leaps the tarpon, chief of salty game.

Come, then, dear anglers, tourists, haste to share The bounteous feasts by this new Journal spread ; Then turn to seek fair scenes depicted here By surf and stream through angling ardor led.

THE ANGLER'S DELIGHTS.

'Mid scenes of beauty the angler moves,
Follows the river's silver course, Knows all its windings to the sea,
Knows its meanders from its source. Knows all the leapings that it fakes
In bold cascade and waterfall.
Bubbling o'er rapids in career
With roaring voice or mellow call.
He knows the solitude of its depths,
Its sparkling o'er each shallow route,
Knows where to seek the sable bass
And where the flashing, springing trout.
He welcomes Nature when she laughs
With budding groves and flowers of spring
With violet flowers and dew-wet grass And sumptuous orchards blossoming ;
The rustling sedges music make;
The robins, meadow-larks pipe sweet :
The brown thrush and the bobolink With soft, melodious chantings greet.
He throws the line when autumn time Flashes the skies and woods with light,
When orchards bend with golden fruits And fields with harvest grain are bright.
And when the winter snows lie deep Forth to some summer clime he hies,
     Where Florida is red with flowers And warm'd by semi-tropic skies.
     There in that glowing land forgets
The storms that lash his northern shore,
Loving to tread the orange groves,
That Eden Paradise explore.
There casts his line in broad lagoon
Or where the mangrove isles expand, For channel bass, crevalle or drum,
For grouper or the tarpon grand.

THE ANGLER'S PLEASURES.

The angler's joys we celebrate—the sports That lure him from tumultuous scenes of life, That win him from the city's noisy street,

From mart, from wharf, from avaricious strife. T aey lead him forth to Nature's loveliest scenes, Where he can roam in meditative mood, Can muse by margin of the sparkling stream Or linger in the shadows of the wood.

How pure, refined, their dear delights must be Who with instructed eye these scenes survey, When dawning's first effulgence o'er them steals. Or twilight's roseate blushes o'er them play.

Their upturn'd eyes with transport and with awe The grand sublimities of Nature view,

The peaks mountainous with their crowns of snow, The torrents storming the wild ravines through. There shaggy forests frown o'er each abyss, The dusky hemlocks and the shivering pines ; And in swift eddies whirling o'er the rocks, They cast with cunning hand the spinning line.

They walk thro' meadows blazing thick with
blooms,

They track the wimpling brook thro' thickets green,

Their senses thrill with rapture as they gaze. Their minds are tone'd harmonious with the scene.

They list with tranquil joy each rural sound,

The low of herds, the mill wheel's pleasing hum,

The village bells—the songs of harvest field, The melodies of bird-choirs, never dumb.

O'er the blue bay as dreamily they float

They note all beauties of the woodland shore, And by the borders of the sounding sea

They list the breaker's voice, the billow's roar. 'Mid such fair scenes the purest influence dwells, Where images of peace the soul pervade On Nature's bosom they find perfect rest.

All griefs and sorrows of the world allay'd.

THE ANGLER'S LOVE OF THE WOODS.

Dear to the angler's heart the shadowy groves. Whose leafy branches droop above the stream. Some full-brimm'd river sweeping on its way, Now dim in shade and now bright in gleam.

They greet, they beckon him with all their leaves, They welcome him with silences and sound. Their birds with swelling operas invite,
Their wild flowers all his wandering steps surround.

He seeks the woods that hem St. Lawrence Gulf. And there, where rush the waters to the deep. He casts the shining fly with nervous hand, And takes the lordly salmon as they leap.

He seeks the depths of Adirondack wilds,
Where the primeval forests weave their shades ; And there his barbed hook and pliant rod

Take springing trout from ripples and cascades. Dear to the angler's heart the far-spread lake. Encircled dense with groves of living green, Where willows dip their tassels in the wave And oak and hemlock form impervious screen.

Dear to the angler's heart the rivulet's flow, That winds and sparkles thro' the grassy mead. Its banks enamell'd with the wilding flower, Its roses red, its water-lilies pale.

Dear to the angler's heart the old mill pond, With its still deeps, its fall of foamy white, For t..ere, o'er pebbly shoal and sandy bar, The snining fishes glitter in his sight.

When by the river or the brooklet stream,
With all their gloom, with all their changeful gleam,
With their soft prattle and their joyous play, How swift pass moments of each lovely day !

THE ANGLER'S DAY.

" There is no life more pleasant than the life of the well--governed angler."—
haak Walton.

Equipt with rod and reel and creel.
Forth to the river side I pass Ere yet the crimson orb of day
Touches the leaves and dewy grass:
I saunter down the shaded lane,
Haste o'er the meadow green,
Then pause beneath a drooping tree.
That yields its friendly screen ;
And here unseen I scan the stream,
Its ripples and still deeps.
To note where lurk the dusky bass
And where the big trout leaps.
And when the sun peeps o'er the hill,
All nature is awake,
The song birds tune their tinkling lyres
In thicket, bush and brake:
The robin on the elm branch sings,
The meadow lark on sprays.

And all the fluttering, feather'd choir
Their matin anthems raise.

The wind is sweet with breath of flowers,
Soft sighs it thro' the wood ;
Fair sights, sweet sounds delight the sense, To charm the angler's mood.
He casts his silken braided line
Where eddies o'er the pebbles boil,
Wherc ripples and the foam bells sweep
O'er rock beds in turmoil :
He casts where dim and deep the stream
Flows 'neath the Cerhanging bank, Where wild red roses cluster thick
And golden rods grow rank :
And oft his tempting fly cloth lure,
And oft the barbel hooks secure I

THE BROOK OF AULD LANG SYNE.

As months and rolling years depart.

And human lives decline,

With an intenser love the heart

Clingeth to auld lang syne ; Though costly roof and gilded dome

Above us brightly shine,

Still do we cherish childhood's home.

The roof of auld lang syne!

We love the song of piping bird,

Sheep bleat and low of kine.

For hymn of bird and sounds of herd

Remind of auld tang syne.

We love at dawn's encrimson'd break

Thro' grove of cak or pine

To pass, for near them gleams the lake

And brook of auld lang syne.

Ah! happy time, enchanting time!

When first with rod and line,

We hasten'd in the sweet June time

To   brooks of auld lang sayne ; Where shadows of the branching oak

Made   dim the tranquil stream.

Where bright the spangled beauties broke

With such resplendent gleam !

We knew each sandy bar and cove.

Each rock where ripples spun,

Each shallow where the lilies throve,

Each reach where currents run ;

We knew where 'neath each green bank side

Where red the roses twine,

In hollow'd cave the darlings hide,

The trout of auld lang syne!

SCENES THAT GREET THE ANGLER.

Deep amid the arching woods
It is pleasant to recline.
When the dewey twinkling leaves With the early sunbeams shine ;
Then the bending grass around Fringing the embowering glade,
Gleams, as if with diamonds sown, Or with Orient pearls inlaid. Fragrant then the breath of morn, Wafting over dew-wet fields,
Where each lowly herb that springs
Grateful incense lavish yields.
And each blooming wildwood flower, Lovely, graceful. as it bends
To the wooing breeze a dower
Of the choicest odor lends.
By the hedges that skirt the way, Thick the pink-hued wild rose grows.
By the margin of the brook,
Red the Cardinal blossom glows. In the meadow's verdant lap,
Thick the scarlet strawberries bloom,
And their soft, delicious scent Yields the sweetest of perfume,
Countless as the stars of heaven Are the purple violets spread.
Pouring from their honied cups Incense o'er the grassy bed.
Deep amid those shady woods
It   is   pleasant to recline,
When the sultry bearns of noon
O'er the swooning woodlands shine.
Then beneath some thick-leaved beech,
Or a pine tree's dusky shade
Or a willow's drooping bower, Pleasant is your refuge made.
When a shadow is o'er the stream. And a ripple crisps its face.
Soft and silent be your tread.
At your favorite angling place. Then with deftest skill you cast Silken line and feather'd lure, Soon your creel is filling f .st
With the spangled, brilliant spoil, Rich reward for all your toil.

SPRINGTIME FISHING.

The spring day. the spring day. When blossoms ope around. When in the wood and on the hill

Flowers decorate the ground ;

When down the brook the angler seeks The spangled, finny kind, And schoolboys climb the orchard tree The bluebird's nest to find ; And o'er the fields the sower casts The grain seeds all about, And in the furrow'd glebe is heard The plowman's cheery shout.

Ah ! spring day, wide-blossoming spring day !

I love the dewy, bright spring day,

You know where 'neath.the mill-dam-fall

The yellow perch schools gleaming skim , You know where, 'mid the lily-pads, The pickerel near the surface swim ; Then stand where weeping willows shake Their drooping tassels o'er the pool. And cast the silken braided line Amid the thickest of the school. And soon triumphant with the toil

You homeward hasten with your spoil.

The angler, too, of riper years

Will seek the shores of sea-like Sound. Equipt with fine artistic gear, To seek the bass in depths profound. To cast his glittering lure to take The bluefish leaping from the brine. Or shapely weakfish of the seas, With humming reel and whistling line.

THE FISHERMAN'S ILL LUCK.

An angler casts his braided line
Fast by a brooklet's grassy edge ; Alas, his hook caught in a root,
His line was tangled in the sedge. When it was free he cast again,
Hopeful a spangled trout to snare, Alas, a worthless bull-pout came,
Struggling, convulsive in the air. An angler by a crystal lake
Sought eager for a black-bass prize ; Alas upon his hook impaled.
A writhing sunfish meets his eyes! An angler by the river's bank,
Whose golden willows cast a shade,
Hoped there a salmon, large and bright,
Would snatch the glittering lure displayed ; Alas, a humble pickerel
His only prey for rod and reel
An angler by Floridian stream,
Zealously sought the tarpon king; He cast his line with Matchless skill,
His reel did hum, his line did sing : There came a dash, a mighty splash,
He thought the kingly fish his game. Alas, 'twas channel-bass that came! An angler by the ccean surf,
Cast 'for a bluefish far his line, Or for a Spanish mackerel,
Careering thro' the foamy brine : Alas, a dogfish rises there,
The sole reward for skill and care ; Or sculpin or the long-tail skate,
Seize greedily his tempting bait ! In ripples of the breezy bay,
He sought the weakfish for his creel; Alack those darlings failed to bite, He only caught a slippery eel!

THE CATFISH *(Primelotus Catus).*

Deep and tranquil the millpond lies, Dark where shaded by cloudy skies Yet glassy bright and crystal clear When sunshine gilds the atmosphere. By bushy bank and grassy shore Graceful the willow trees lean o'er, Loving their twinkling leaves to dip, Loving the cooling waves to sip : The splendid cardinal flowers illume Its borders with their scarlet bloom ; The water lilies on its breast Like fairy shallops at anchor rest.

And there beneath their floating screen The pond fish wander and lurk unseen. And there in each free holiday

The angling school boys seek their prey. The catfish, bullhead, horned pout, Love not the clear brook of the trout. But in the sluggish pond or lake Their homes in deep abysses make, And there in shadowy places hide, To snare the shiners as they glide.

There school child comes with tackle rude, Invading their lone solitude.

Best is their sport when evening's shade The sluggish current doth prevade, For then the eels and catfish bite, More eager in the glooms of night.

In far Missouri's river tide

The greedy " lady catfish " glide ; Of heavy weight, symmetric frame. They sweep the channels for their game : Then chub and roach and minnow fry Before those ravenous monsters fly. So swift in speed, so hard to kill, They task the angler's deftest skill. Defying in the channel's stress His vain endeavors at success.

16

FISHING IN A MAINE LAKE.

Oh. let us float o'er this pellucid stream, Idling the hours of summer-time away, Let us forget all fashions of the world. Its cares, its fretful griefs. anxieties, Ambitions, pride. and selfish low desires. The greedy struggles of the rich for wealth, The slavish toil of poverty for bread, The arrogance of power, the hard fate Of men in squalid but and cabins rude, And all the sordid passions of mankind.

Onward in birch canoe, we listless float Now in the sunshine, now in shadcws lost. Where a great mountain casts its inky shade. And waves beneath seem fathomless. There is depressing sadness in the glooms

That overspread these streams, and quick we ply The oar, to float in heaven's bright light again ; Toiling at paddle, soon the light canoe Speeds like an arrow, like a flitting bird With scarce a breaking ripple at the stern. Pausing, entranced we downward gaze, Deep in the wave—we note the floating cloud And the pure, blue etherial skies above Reflected, picturing a new heaven below. From a cliff summit, an o'erarching tree Leans o'er, its great inverted form to see. Viewing its tops sink prone beneath. The flapping crows, the circling hawks that pass. Catch their swift wings reflected in the wave ; And high, majestic on a dead tree branch An eagle sits observant of the scene ; A soaring fish-hawk skims across the wave Then drops his wings to seize the finny prey : Zig-zag a kingfisher flies screaming past.

And from the lake comes cry of whooping crane, And melancholy wail of lonely loon. All there the angler notes with dreamy sense. And then anon he takes the tapering rod, And casts the feathered lure with s' ilful hand,

He takes the lordly salmon and the trout
That free in watery abysses float.
The fleeting hours are all too brief for him.
So fitted with pleasing sights and pleasant sounds, So when the evening shades steal gradual round He turns reluctant to his leafy camp.

I ZAAK WALTON.

Two centuries since thy form was seen By river bank and brooklet side,
Where the swift Humber pours its wave And Dove and Derwent currents glide :
By full-brimmed Tweed and tranquil Rye Thou lov'st to cast the line and fly,
Loving dark morn and showery day When dace and perch bit eagerly; Where
down the limpid brook the trout From whirling eddies spring and dash, Where
grayling, carp and bream and pike O'er the swift currents brightly flash, Or
where great salmon of the stream. Amid the foam-bells glide and gleam, Loving
all charming sports that fill The angler's bosom with a thrill! All
anglers of this distant land Love their dear Walton's famous name, Deep 'tis
inscribed on every heart, That throbs responsive to thy fame ; Roamers in
Adirondack woods, In Saranac who cast their hooks. The anglers of the
grand Maine streams, Trout-fishers in Long Island brooks, Fishers in great St.
Lawrence Gulf, Or by the Labrador's bleak coast, Do try for pike and
muscalunge
Where Northern lakes by gales are toss'd ; The anglers of remotest West,
Who take the pickerel and bass, All think of thee with loving heart, The
father of the angling art..

WALTON ON THE PLEASURES OF ANGLING.

" Let me live tranquil," dear old Walton said, Reclined in shade of honeysuckle hedge ; In placid rest his present pastime o'er. On a green bank fast Dy the river's edge. How sweet the pastime of the angler's art! Rejoicing in past hours not idly spent After the anxious toils of busy life

Happy the task and perfect the content. It is a cheerer of the spirits dull.

Solace in sadness and of troubled mind:

It calms the passions as it soothes the soul. Dispelling ills that agitate mankind ;

Begets sweet moods of patience and of peace In those 'hat practice this supremest art ; Teaches the virtues of humility,

And all the blessings that delight the heart. "Let me live tranquil " by the grassy brink Of Trent or Avon, happy in my soul,

And watch my angle in the eddies play.

Or where in deeps the sluggish currents roll. Sitting at rest I view the wondrous scenes Of nature 'round me bounteous display'd,

At morning's blush. in evening's dim approach, When twilight glimmerings blend with dusky shade. All the deep groves make music in the leaves, Their flutterings fill with whisperings the air : The birds attune their liquid melodies, And charm each soul disturb'd by earthly care. Soft. pleasing fancies fill my soul entranc'd. As I the woodlands and the waters view; The grassy pastures and the meadows green, Thick-sown with daisies and the violets blue. I note the streams careering to the sea.

The rivulets brown, the brooks with sparkling face, And see the silver-scald fish disport,

Whirling in schools, swift-darting in the race. And while I view these charms of waves and air, These wonders of the great Creator's hand, My soul forsakes this sublunary sphere

To soar o'er upper skies to heavenly land.

Dear, loving angler ! though two hundred years Have strewn the dust above thy earthly frame, Yet memories of thy faultless life abide.

And in the angler's heart survives thy fame ; Garlands of love around thee we entwine, Undying wreaths affectionate we bring: Remembrance of thy pure, unruffled life Eternally to angler's mind will cling!

IZAAC WALTON'S COMPLETE ANGLER'S –
RETREAT.

It was a quiet old inn of ancient times, With faded sign-board swinging at the door. With ivies and rare wisterias cover'd o'er; Sweet-smelling fields encircled it about.

An humble garden rich with shrubs and flowers, An apple orchard drooping with its fruit, Lilacs and rosebush weaving a green bower; A gray old church, embower'd in aged trees. Unprais'd its ivied tower and belfry near :

While here and there a moss-roof'd cottage stood Embrown'd by suns and rains of many a year. Hard by a river wound its tranquil course. Reflecting from its face o'er-bending trees, Fill'd with gay songsters of the earth and air, That trill'd forever their sweet melodies ; A rustic bridge the narrow river spann'd, A time-stain'd mill revolved its dripping wheel ; Green, grassy meadows stretch'd their billowy

space

Till lost in distance, far as eye might steal ; A peaceful spot. where passions of the world, Its stormy strifes, anxieties and cares. Might ne'er disturb the quiet of the mind. To fill with anguish those sojourning there.

Yes. by this placid river sweeping past,

And 'neath the shadows of those ancient trees,

Lull'd by the liquid anthems of the birds, The robin's chirp, the blackbird's harmonies. Dear Walton ever had supreme delight, A guest thrice welcome into Nature's round. In Nature's music no discordant chord Jars on the senses with disturbing sound, Her beauteous face a smile forever wears

To fill the soul with peace. unvex'd with cares. There in the trellised arbor of the place, The angler sat in meditative mood.

Sooth'd by the gentle murmur of the stream, Sooth'd by the whisper'd voices of the wood, When clouded skies a dusky shadow throw Athwart the winding reaches of the tide. Casting an inky blackness o'er the deeps. Or where the rippling eddies whirling glide. He stood with pliant rod and tackle fine, And deftly cast the gry. illusive fly.

Took leaping trout and sable-armor'd bass. Or pickerel where amid the pads they lie. And so the days slip pleasantly away, The rosy mornings and the evenings gray. Each moment precious, and each hour a joy, Each sight a bliss, each sound a choral hymn

WALTON'S CONVERSE WITH AN ANGLER.

Dear angler, musing by this placid stream,

List to the thoughts that have posess'd my soul. That you may join with me in thankfulness

For all the blessings that have crown'd our lives: Consider the calamities we have 'scap'd;

Each misery we miss is mercy new.

Others have met with most disastrous woes, With broken limb or sickness unto death

But we've been free from fatal miseries

That vex mankind—so let us thankful be!

Nay, from accusing conscience we've been free, Then heaven he praised for such protecting grace !Ah ! there be those of rich domains possess'd. Who'd gladly give their opulence of gold,

Healthful and cheerful like ourselves to be, Who, having little of this world's estates, Have sung, rejoic'd and angled by the streams. Yes, there be those of grasping, miserly soul Who think that wealth true happiness confers.

Yet spare us, heaven, from poverty and want. So we may be with competence content.

Let none repine, or envy men of wealth,

For cares that are the keys of hoarded gold So heavy hang at girdle of the rich.

They crush with heavy weight their burden'd lives. Rich men too oft are vex'd with cares, to keep The boundless wealth, dishonorably got,

So thankful be for competence and health!

Hail to the jocund Spring, when orchards bloom, Clematis, honeysuckles, white and pink,

Pour cataracts of blossoms far and wide ;

When aureate light swims o'er the valleys green, Mosses and lichens everywhere upspring.

Daisies and buttercups the rivulets fringe,

And the wild roses' crimson petals ope;

When new-born grasses spread a verdurous screen : Then from the banks where sweep the currents by We'll cast the silken line and painted fly.

.   .   .   .

Welcome, pure thoughts, and welcome, budding groves,

The springing grass, the spicy, opening buds Welcome, the tuneful birds that chant their hymns Perch'd on the thickets, fluttering o'er each spray ; Welcome, sweet Peace, that in these woodland-dells Dwells where no hateful passions may invade ; Welcome, each winding brook of crystal flow, In whose smooth mirror shine

21

reflected skies ; In whose calm deeps or ruffled eddies glide The silvery fishes darting thro' the tide ;

For here is angler's paradise supreme,
The flowing river, the transparent stream.

THATWIN FATHERS.

Izaak Walton, Father of British Anglers. Seth Green, Father of American I' i,hers.

Musing, dear Walton, on thy tranquil life. The parent angler of the lake and stream, Father of anglers in thy native land, I conjure up thy form in fancy's dream. Long musing still another gracious Sire,

Our own Seth Green, thrills all my heart with pride; Who lov'd and taught the angler's gentle art, Sought to replenish each depleted tide. But now his kindly bosom throbs no more, His silver'd brow 'neath mossy marbles prest, Beyond the unknown river he hath pass'd, Wafted to regions of eternal rest !

We grace thy bust with bright, memorial crown, Perennial laurel, emblem of thy fame, And on the altar of our loving heart, Inscribe in memory thy beloved name. Lover of Nature—ever thou did'st find. Beauties that all the natural world might boast, In azure skies, in woods in mountains grand.

In valley-streams, in surges of the coast. No eye more true to mark swift-flying bird, No hand more firm the volleying shot to pour, No skill more perfect with the tapering rod, By sparkling brooklet or by ocean shore. In all the brotherhood of Angling Art

How deep the sorrow that thou should'st depart I Belove'd Walton ! Though two hundred years Have cast their ashes o'er thy place of rest, Still thy fond children in profoundest love. Cherish the name that is supremely blest.

Pure thy career. with tranquil pleasures crown'd.
Happy thy life in peaceful pastimes spent,

By full-brimm'd Tweed, or rushing Derwent's tide, By famous Avon, or by lovely Trent. No earthly passions vexed thy thoughtful mind, No love of gain, no thirst for sordid gold. No love for gilded fashions of the world.

No love for strifes or warlike flags unroll'd ;
Thy sole enchantments were the sparkling stream. The boiling eddies, where the salmon leap'd,
The wimpling brooks where trout and graylings
glanc'd;
Rich harvest of the waves, by anglers reap'd. Content withal such innocent delights,
With conscience pure, and love of all mankind, Thou had'st no evil passions to subdue ;
'Mid pains and sorrows never yet repin'd.
So like transparent streams thy earthly years, Slip by unvex'd by rough, tempestuous tides, Each passing year unruffled as the flow
Where calm and smooth the mirror d river glides. So, as the glorious sun at

close of day
Sinks in the west, thy life did fade away.

PROLIFIC STREAMS OF AFRICA.

In the dark continent of Afric land

Where Stanley, Speke and Livingstone explor^ed. Where ranged wild game, the quagga. eland race, The panther shriek'd, the tawny lion roar'd, The daring hunters found supremest sport

Slaying the giraffe and the elephant,

Tracking in swamps the hippopotami,

And the rhinoceros in his dismal haunt.

Many the perils these stout heroes met

Baker and Cumming, and brave Du ChailluMartyrs to science and to Christian cause,

Who well have pictur'd all the scenes they knew ; Their deadly conflicts and their triumphs grand, With the swart natives ravaging the land.

Yet came no angler to explore the depths

Of foaming river and transparent stream

To lure the finny treasures that they held ;

The hues, the shapes that thro' the waters gleam—Brave Stanley, Livingstone. explored those wastes Of waters—Nyanza, Tanderagas' deeps ;

Sailed the broad Congo, Combe and the Nile, Sangora's lake, and where the Timlah sleeps ; Yet left no record of the finny tribes.

Great schools to civilized man unknown ;

No angling rod they bore—the rifle-gun

Their sole companion in that torrid zone.

Yet, with coming years, when Christian creed With rule intrepid brightens all the land ;

When Arab slavers cease their fiendish work. And villas rise where reed-thatch'd cabins stand : When white-wing'd squadrons sweep the ocean shore,

And steaming trains thro' trackless forests glide, And forest life is safe by mount and stream ;

As commerce spreads its influence far and wide, Then will the angler reap a fresh delight By flowing river and the torrent-I·all,

Seeking new victims to his rod and ree!, New fields of pastime open unto all.

THE MEADOW AND WOODLAND STREAMS.

It is a lovely, transparent stream. Rippling and flashing with sudden gleam. Where it flows thro' a wide, unshadowed space. Fair as a maiden's smiling face:

For here no thickets or tangled hedge. No drooping grove at the water's edge. May cast a vapory, dusky shade On wheeling current or white cascade.

So here at the meadow's open bank.

Where reeds and rushes spring green and rank. The angler comes with tackle fine. To spin the reel and cast the line : Where ripples sparkle and eddies sport. There in their gambols gleam the trout ; They dive in deeps, the surface skim. O'er sandy shallows they leap and swim And sunfish glitter with shiny sides, The yellow perch with swiftness glides. And where the lily-pads spread a sheet. The pickerel lurk *in* dim retreat. So here in this calm, pellucid stream, The angler's ecstasy is supreme.

But where a river runs dark and deep. Great hemlock trees around it sweep : The gloomy spruce and sombre pine. With pendant branches the borders line. And ever a solemn spell doth brood O'er inky waters and silent wood.

When twilight glimmers, weird and dim. And mystical shapes in ether swim, 'Tis said a spectre, tall and grim, Haunteth an old mill by the stream.

It enters that olddoor,

At dusty window it seems to kneel

It leans o'er the dripping water-wheel. It wrings its hands, and sad and slow, With soundless footsteps, to and fro.

It paces o'er the floor.

Now, oft at rising of a gale.

A shrill, mysterious, solemn wail

Swells in that lonely place ;

Then sudden that phantom plunges down Where whirls the river's current brown—

Plunges and leaves no trace.

26

THE MASCALONGE AND THE PICKEREL.

'Mid inlets, wood-embowered and green. Like emeralds dropped in waves of blue,
The angler floats at break of day,
Quick paddling there his birch canoe.
There, high on drooping boughs entwin'd, The grapevine weaves its leafy wealth,
Or drops its purple clusters down
To dip in waves that flow beneath.
The red-bird from the topmost branch Outpours its mellow burst of song ;
The larks and beach birds of the shore Their soft, harmonious trills prolong.
And when the evening shades prevail The whippoorwill repeats its tale.
•

There is the fisher's Paradise,
A dream-like, Eden-like retreat, 'Mid balmy perfumes of the air,
And wildflowers springing at his feet.
The floating fish, gay-hued are seen Slow-drifting. now 'mid lilypads.
Now in unfathom'd depths serene.
There *Esox Luciodes* dwells.
With bristling teeth and open jaw.
Insatiate, savage, swift to seize The prey that fills his hungry maw.
And   here the angler's utmost skill
Is   tasked the struggling fish to kill, To land him, gasping and supine.
With whirling wheel and swinging line.
Far where Ontario's waters chafe
The rocky bluffs that line the shore,

Where the Canadian meadows stretch
And crystal rivulets outpour,
The savage mascalonge doth roam,
No rival in his blue domain, No rebel to disturb his home.
E'en as the lion of the waste Appals the desert with his tread.
And all the lesser creatures fly At menace of his shaggy head,
So doth the ruthless mascalonge Despotic rule the watery way,
So the weak fishes of the deep Affrighted vanish from his sway. Where the broad
Huron rolls its wave, And where Superior, thro' the Strait Of Mackinaw, hurls
out its tide, The mascalonges swiftly glance
Thro' fathomless, far-rolling deeps, Far thro' the limitless expanse,
Far as the boiling current sweeps.

THE LUMINOUS BAIT.

Dear angler, equipt with rod and reel, The luminous bait. the ample creel, Haste forth to the rushing river-tide. Where ripples glitter, where fishes glide. And cast with skill your luring fly When the light of day illumes the sky ; Ah, then there's a new delight for him. A pastime fresh as day grows dim, For then. as denser the shadows grow, The luminous bait a gleam will throw, Illuming the waters dimmed by night, And reveal to fishes allurements bright ;

Then gay phosphorescence will flush the stream, Disclosing the depths with sudden gleam. And then you may reap, in evening tide. A harvest of fish in day denied. Since years when old Walton cast the bait, In tranquil Dove, or Derwent's tide. Some new allurements the angler's art Receives by brooklet and riverside ; The perfect Orvis whirling reel

Will cheer the angler with rich prize, And bring abundance to willow-creel. Where grand St. Lawrence currents sweep Men take the salmon in their deep, The pike, the pickerel of the lake, The blackfish and the trout they take ; But when the evening shades prevail.

And darkness gathers o'er mount and va'e. 'Tis then the shining, luminous spoon. Will take the fish beneath the moon ! So when the brilliant Summer days Are sunbright with the noonday rays, The luminous, gay-colored bait

Attracts the fishes to their fate ;

Though then the waters are blurred with stain, And other lures may tempt in vain, This wondrous, shining luminous lure, The hungry victims will secure

They take them either when day is dim, Or when fresh sunbright waves they swim.

TROUTING.

The season is ended—the rod and the reel With affectionate care are hung on the wall, Yet still that symmetrical rod we may see
And its joys and successes recall ;
As we gaze the woodlands of June-time revive,
They are fluttering with all their green leaves.
They are glad with the songs of the musical birds,
They are bright with the light the umbrage re-ceives;
The orchards we pass are resplendent with bloom,
The meadows we tread are with flowerets inlaid, The brooks are embroidered with emerald grass
As they leap into light or darken in shade ; We see in each ripple the flash of a fin,
And where minnows turn up their silvery sides We see the swift dart of speckel'd brook trout ; Like an arrow among them he glides.
Ah, there's a dim pool beneath the mill-wheel
Where the depths are ne'er churned into foam, And there, 'neath the roots of an old oak tree,
I know the big trout have a home
Then cautious thy step and steady thy hand,
Let thy shadow fall not o'er the wave.Let thy line circle o'er with delicate cast
And with a brief struggle the captive you save. There's a brook that- flows down at the skirt of the hill,
It laughs and it prattles and it chatters with glee : It sweeps over pebbles, it glides over sands, It kisses the roots of sapling and tree ;
Now is lost in the bushes that tangle the shore.
Now check'd by the grasses that border its sides, Now again it leaps forth where no tree-shade may fall,
As sparkling and riotous onward it glides ;
And there may the angler's allurement of flies
Sweep the brook and secure the coveted prize.
There's a creek that flows up from the blue, salty
bay,

It winds thro' the sedges and marshes at will ; The plovers and beach-birds skim o'er its face. ' And the sickel-curlews whistle wildly and shrill. There upward it runs to freshen its tides
Where Massapeaque Lake to the sea loweth down, And there swim the sea-trout with silvery dyes, As brilliant as gems in an emperor's crown And there with my friend, Genio Scott, in past year, In the long-vanish'd year we gather'd the prize. The treasures, the pleasures, to angler so dear.

WHEN AND WHERE TO ANGLE FOR TROUT.

Dear angler, haste to your favorite stream That flows transparent. with sudden gleam. In open space where the blue of sky Looks down as gentle as maiden's eye. Where the rippling eddies whirling bright Sweep over sand-bars. crystal white, For there in the wheeling, sparkling tide, The spotted trout-schools like meteors glide.

Or seek some shaded nook serene Where alder thickets o'er it lean, And the willows droop to see below Their imag'd forms in the waters' flow, For there in the tranquil, slumberous deeps The springing trout o'er the surface leaps. Pursuing the silvery minnow race Or insects, skimming th' unruffled space ; So, there cast far your feather'd lure, The wilful victims to secure.

Or seek some upland's secluded shore. Where riotous rivulets downwards pour, Streamlets sprung from crystaline foul t Far up some rocky, snow-clad mount ; Laughing, rejoicing, as quick they leap, Joyous, and active as forth they sweep. For in each toss of the creamy foam They find an ice-cold, grateful home ;

And there the angler's delusive flies Entice, entrap the speckled prize.

Or haste to some pond serene and large By lilies fring'd at the grassy marge. Where red wild-roses stoop to lave There cluster'd garlands in the wave, For there in shadow'd and tideless space The lurking trouts have hiding   place. There eager they seize the tempting bait—And soon they fill the creel with weight.

THE TROUT BROOK.

Under the willow's twisted root,
With hollow murmur, with suddon shoot Thro' shady thicket and grassy nook.
Floweth the running brook; Now in shadowy gloom it runs, Where never shine the summer suns ;
Now it leaps into light again, Singing ever a joyous strain : Rippling. twinkling. glittering ever, Down to the brimming river.
Now in a calm lagoon it sleeps. Lazily, drowsily on it creeps.
Scarcely seen to flow ; There the water lilies float. Each one like a silver boat,
There the cresses grow ;
By the water on mossy stone
Or slippery log, with weeds o'ergrown.
The spotted turtles lie,
Or sudden slip in the pool of glass, Affrighted when the cattle pass.
Or steps the intruder by.
Yet best 1 love the noisy stream
When it bursts with cheerful laugh and gleam Into open land, beneath the beam
Of bright. unclouded day :

Twinkling, glimmering in the sun. As if rejoicing its race to run On its merry way
Over the sands of golden glow, Over pebbles white as snow.
It tumbles and it glides.
There swim the perch and the dusky bream. The speckled trout. like meteors gleam. Shooting across the limpid stream,
I lashing their purple sides ;
Anl there the angler comes to play With silken line the lurking prey,
Th.:: school-child hither hastes to glean The water cresses crisp and green, Or comes the bard to ponder o'er The tranquil beauties of the shore.

TROUT BROOK GLEN.

1 love this bowery spot,

With leafage multitudinous o'er head,

A pastoral, fairy grot,

Where fabled wood nymphs might delight to tread ; Where ever is sweet sound

Of brooks descending from the hills,

Thro' moor and meadow ground ; Gurgling and laughing with delicious trills. Now shooting o'er smooth passages of sand, Now gushing thro ravines on either hand,

To cast their tributes in the limpid pool

So shadowed and so cool !

Athwart the water's face. Branch-shadows and leaf-shadows love to sleep, Where beams of sunlight thro' the umbrage deep

Illumine all the place.

Bright shafts of light that thro' the foliage gleam To gild the embrowned surface of the stream.

In this enchanting grot

I lingering forget the outside world of life,

All griefs, anxieties forgot

Forgot all tumult and the endless strife, As I but list the murmur of the stream And sighing of the breeze,

Noting the sifting, evanescent gleam

Of sunlight thro' the trees

I hear the mellow hymns of singing birds,

The hum of bees. the lowing of the herds.

And all the lulling sound

Of nature in repose profound

But sweetest to my ear the sudden splash, Where the swift trout across the ripples dash. And pleasing then the glitter of their sides As each sharp fin the wave divides. Where o'er the crystal pool they leap To seize the hovering insects in their sweep.

A TROUT BROOK AND A PLEASANT SPOT IN THE WOODS.

It was a lovely haunt, set like a gem
In the dim shadows of o'erhanging groves, A sylvan Eden where 'twas sweet to muse, Forgetting all vexations of the world. Here mosses soft lay like a carpet spread. In this green sanctuary of the dell,
Where ivies and the pink arbutus grew, Embroidering the banks with tendrils thick. And thick inlaid with purple violets.
Wild honeysuckles perfum'd all the air, With hazel-bush and larch-trees canopied ; And grape-vines threw their garlands prodigal Forming an arbor, dense with grateful shade—Dense with their flowery tufts and pendant leaves. Sweet brier-roses, flowering in the shade, Wove a dim canopy of buds and blooms, O'erspreading the low hillocks of the moss.
While musing here, how natural came the thought Of those wild tribes that once had here a home!

Here a bright brook ran thro' the sylvan shade, Rippling, rejoicing on its bubbling way Here boiling o'er the pebbles of the strand.
That paved with crystal stones the brooklet floor Anon with sluggish course it wound its way. Slipping unwrinkled o'er the yellow sand. It was a sweet, calm paradise that lured The patient angler. for his pastime sport So, here he cast the line and feathered lure, That skimmed the eadies or the placid deeps, Enticing the bright trout to seize the bait, Snaring the struggling victims to their fate ! Such a rare Eden for the angler's art Would sure have won old Walton's gentle heart.

SALMON FISHING.-CHARLES HALLOCK.

0 veteran angler ! ancient friend, Again thy graphic page displays
The wonders of the natural world, The grandeur of the forest-ways.
The sylvan glories of the wood.
Where drooping branches hem the stream
Those sweeping currents, shaded now. Now flashing with a sudden gleam.
'Tis his delight to track the brook
That laughs and prattles down the mead.
To lure the spangled, springing trout. Or pickerel darting from the weed: He
loves, too, by the wood-girt lake. For dusky bass to cast the line,
Or by salt billows of the shore,
To whirl the bluefish from the brine ;
Or far out in profoundest deeps. To drop for sea-bass baited lure,
Or by thy green shores, Florida, The channel-bass prize to secure: Or sturdily
the great rod swing For tarpon, the farn'd Silver King!
But nobler. regal trophy crowns,
With laurel wreath the angler's brow, Who swings the rod and casts the line.
Where swift Canadian rivers flow : Where royal Restigouche pours out. Its
grand, majestic sweep of tide: Or where Saint Lawrence Gulf receives Its
tributaries. deep and wide, Or where Aroostook dashes free To the
tide-waters of the sea Or where New Brunswick like a gem Soars upward
from the encircling brine. Studded with sparkling brooks and lakes. Encrown'd by
forest-wilds of pine The angler finds a joy supreme. By boiling river,
rushing stream.
By wind-swept cliff and jutting bar. Where circling eddies swirl and wheel, He
sees the mighty salmon spring. He hears the music of his reel: He
contemplates with strange delight, Those rivers riotous and deep Some
dash to sea in headlong way. Some sinuous loiter as they sweep. Some
upward leap in creamy foam, Some plunge and tumble in abyss, Some flow
past with a murmuring note. Or lion's roar, or serpent's hiss ; But ever 'mid
the spume and spray, The lordly salmon speed their way!

" One of the charms of angling is that it presents an endless teld for argument,
speculation, and experiment.-
—T. E. Pere T.

SALMON WATERS.

Grand are those Northern streams where salmon schools
Leap in abysses of the currents bright,
Broad streams whose wilful and capricious moods Give to the angler a supreme delight. There fish are full of energy and life Where there is sparkling, brilliancy of foam. But where in waters dead repose the waves; The fish are sluggish in their lifeless home. Some streams dash swiftly without break to sea, Some creep in slow and sinuous career,
Some have great depth and breadth in headlong
sweep,
Some in pent up channels madly steer. Glorious are they hemmed with granite rocks, Resplendent with the ever flashing spray : Encircled close by vivid evergreens, Sombre in shadows of the cloudy day ;
Yet bright and sparkling in the clear sunbeam, Delighting all that angle in the stream, Rippled by gusty winds of wanton sweep, Or swirl of leaping salmon of the deep.

In long past years those unsought rivers ran, Known to but few as they incessant flow'd, Their forest glooms unscored by swamper's ax, Their haunts sequestered showed no loggers' road ; But now that wilderness by steam is cross'd. The calm and romance of the woods are lost.
The anglers oft their other triumphs boast, Slaying the mighty tarpon of the
deep, Gaffing the striped-bass from ocean rocks,
Thinning the trout-schools as they flashing leap, But yet no fish is of the salmon peer. In its wild haunts, its wonderful career.
In some streams, spacious, frequent are the pools Glinting with pebbles, open to the light. Others are short, tumultuous in their flow, Checked by rough boulders in their arrowy flight.Some are o'erhung with densest shade of woods, Whose branches cast a shadow o'er the wave ; Others slip past at base of barren cliffs.
Whose rocky walls the rushing billows lave.

SALMON POOLS.

The salmon fishing in Canadian streams Is fair as that enjoyed on foreign shores,
The scenery more majestic. streams more grand. And our great salmon of the
noblest size. To pass o'er regions of St. Lawrence shores, Gives to the mind
seclusion from the world. Here one can contemplate the soaring mounts. The
majesty of broad, impetuous streams. The whirl of salmon, antics of the
seals, And all the brilliancies of northern skies. The gorgeous wonder of
the lunar bow, So the wide world no fairer scenes presents Than by the
billows of Columbia's shores. In some streams frequent. ample are the tides,
Open to sunlight, sown with pebbles bright, Others are short, tumultuous in
their flow. Check'd by huge boulders in their foamy flight, Many are dim with
densest shades of woods. Whose branches cast broad shadows o'er the wave, While
others rush by base of jutting cliffs. Whose rocky walls the angry waters
lave. Grand are the Goodbout pools, tumultuous streams, Bright with the ever-
glancing, leaping spray ; Glorious are they in their varied scenes. Inclosed by
groves of sombre evergreens. Lovely. these pools, when sparkling in the light,
Entrancing in their perfect solitudes: Stirred only by the wind or
salmon whirls, Or dimmed by floating cloud, or leafy woods Dotted by
verdurous inlets that divide The flowing currents, the careering tides;
Fair are their vistas, opening to the view, Forests, primeval, that
encircling gird The boiling rapids with their yeasty foam, And stretch'd
o'er all spreads heaven's celestial
dome.

SALMON FISHING OF LABRADOR.

By the wild Canadian shore, By the randy Labrador.
By the rocky Mingan isles
And where Anticosti smiles, Countless are the salmon shoals, Leaping where the salt tide rolls.
Rivers, streams, of crystal clearness
Pour thro' that extended strand
From thy river mouth, St. Lawrence,
To the coast of Newfoundland Far as where the Belle-isle S:rait Opens to the seas its gate.
Cold those rivers as the fountains
From the wilderness that flow: Cold as torrents of the mountains.
Gelid with the ice and snow. There. amid the salt abysses Or the river's Springtime tide,
Gleaming, flashing, leaping, diving, Shoals cf noble salmon glide.
Where the river of St. John
Mingles with the ocean surf,
Brown with weedy rocks and sand drifts,
Green with bordering velvet turf, There the angler with his tackle.
When the July suns are high,
From the dawning to the twilight,
Hastes   to   angle with the fly.
Near   thy   alder-skirted border,
Where the Rattling Run doth twine. He erects his but of branches.
Branch of hemlock and of pine Floors it with the cedar saplings.
Fragrant. soft as couch of kings There enjoying forest pastimes
And the sleep that labor brings.

SALMON FISHING IN THE FAR WEST.

In estuaries broad, by rapid fluvial stream,
We pause to note the eddies as they swirl and gleam.
We note the sparkling billows where swift the sea-trout glide
Now plunging in the deep now shooting o'er the tide.
We note the black seals darting, disporting in the flood.
The gray geese with their goslings and wild ducks with their brood.
Anon, see the brown bear fast rushing thro' the fir, Or flocks of speckled partridge as o'er the woods they whir.
Then note the noble salmon, crown'd monarch of the tides
Flashing *in* purple splendor, with ali their burnished sides,
Supreme in stately figure, supreme in matchless hue.
No lovelier fish swims river or cleaves the ocean blue.
That silver king, the tarpon. of Florida the boast, Or speckled bass, bright-armor'd, the glory of the coast,
May all claim wondrous beauty. in salt tides of the sea,
But never may they rival, 0 Royal Salmon, thee ! There where a river pours its cataract adown Subsiding in a pool, all fring'd with boulders brown. On this peninsula, 0 Angler, tal.e now your stand And swing the rod and cast the line with your
strong hand ;
                     So instant in the deep leaps a salmon to the lure
And quick your hook is fast, and the struggling fish secure.
He plunges in affr:ght, he shoots across the stream, He leaps in air with frantic rage. see how his bright sides g'eam

Then vanishing from sight. he sulks in caverns dim, But yields at last, a conquest. that may no longer swim.
Far out in western world, where monarch mountains soar.
While torrents from their summits and rugged ravines pour,
The broad Columbia river, majestic with its tides Through grassy reach of vales and wildernesses glides,
'Tis there the noble salmon in countless numbers pass,
Thro' eddies most tumultuous, or currents clear as glass.

SALMON FISHING IN GOODBOUT RIVER,
CANADA.

The kingly salmon ! what more beautiful, Than his symmetric shape, so fearless fair ! His regal garniture of silvery scales
And flashing eyes resplendent with their light. No marvel that they frolic, leap with joy. Disporting in this cool pellucid stream. Escaping sure from ocean enemies.
Years since were halcyon angling days.
Ere hatching haunts and high leas'd streams were known
Forests were then unscored by swamper's axe, No logging roads invaded regions lone ; No poachers then the forest depths explored And only birch canoes on waves were toss'd. No steam craft sought the unknown wilderness. But now the wilds by railroad trains are cross'd ; And so the wild romance of woods is o'er, And stranger crowds those recesses explore And streams are free to angling rods no more.
We can respect the expert who in his boat The mighty tarpon of the gulf may take.
Or gaff the strip'd bass from the ocean rock,
Or slay the muscalonge in Northern lake ; Yet no fish with the salmon may compare, No other pastime yields such noble sports. For other sports lack mystery of woods.
Lack the rare views of nature's grand resorts. The tarpon is but smasher of the line, Full of rough vigor and of brutal force ;
The strip'd bass fisher sees but sea and surf. He that seeks salmon at the river source Finds endless views 'mid each surrounding scene By shores encircled by the woodlands green, Their play on temper of the stream depends, For where is foam and dash, is energy ;
In the dead water, fish move sluggishly ;
In rapid stream they frolic far and free.
Some streams have depth and breadth and mighty sweep,
Others are pent up, narrow and confined,
Some have broad pools with brightly pebbled floor,
Others have small pools with big boulders lined, Some are o'erhung with thicket and with tree. Some flow 'neath shadows of the precipice. So there's no end to phases of the stream.
No end to angler's skill and artifice!

THE STREAM OF OUR YOUTH.

Stream of our childhood ! 'Twas but a little brook Running thro' reeds with light-hearted laughter ; Seeming far lovelier than river grand,

River of deep vales and bowery woods.

There, rain or shine, our holidays were spent, And well did I know each shallow that it held, Each darkling pool where lurked the spotted trout, And where 'neath lily pads the pickerel lay,

And where the round roaches and shiners had haunt. Its banks with the beech and hickories were lineᵈ. With hemlock and ash and spic'd sassafras. And then, anon, thro' meadows it crept,

Thro' grape-vine tangles devious it wound, And blackberry jungles, until it was lost In sombre forests of cedar and pine.

There sweet birds of song piped tuneful lays ; The robin red-breast with prodigal notes. The upland plovers whistled o'er its banks, The blackbirds pour'd out their souls in song, The kingfisher utter'd its lonely cry,

Bluebird and oriole did hymns unite ;

An' all sweet sounds and fair sights combin'd To charm the angler's senses with delight. There is no stream, however fair it be, Lovely with sandy reach and pebbled shore. Lovely with calm bay, encircled with woods, Where in our later years we made our haunt, That might compare with this enchanted stream That first our early childhood knew and loved.

The river is an emblem of our lives ;

In youth's sweet time we drift thro' pastoral scenes, Flcating by sunny valleys and green meads, To view on shores soft scenes of rural life, Whose flower-enamI'd borders ever glow With beauty, and where youth and pleasure meet And fill with dance and song the blissful hours. Then into wild and passionate life we pass. When vigcrous manhood holds its s'ormy way ; Then, as day ends and life draws near its close, We pass once more through softer. kindlier scenes; Rough scenes of former life left far behind ; Life's turbid waters and life's dangerous reefs Pass'd well safely by—and II is peace again.'

"Some times I go a-fishing and shooting, and even then I carry a note book, that, if I lose game, I may at least bring home some of my pleasant thoughts."

THE POETRY OF ANGLING.

Ah ! who can *number the* bewildering joys That cluster round the angler's pursuit! He follows his rare sport 'mid lovely scenes, Where nature spreads her foliage and her fruit He hastens forth when first the pearly light Of morning flushes all the fields of air ; When first in hazy mounts and tufted wood The sunbeams glitter with effulgence rare. When all the valleys with their flowery plain, When all the forests with their foliage green, Twinkle with dew drops, that the rosy beam Kindles like diamonds on the brow of queen.

The angler tracks the windings of the stream. He knows its leapings in the white cascade, Knows how it bubbles in the rapids swift.

How it sleeps tranquil in each woodland shade ; Knows all the solitudes of its green sides, Knows all the glitter of its shallow tides. He can greet Nature in her spring-time dress, When she trips gleeful thro' the blooming grove ; He can salute in her deep wilderness. As thro' her flowery haunts he loves to rove ; There where the eddies o'er the pebbles spout.

He casts his humming lint and luring flies. 'Mid the swift ripples takes the springing trout Or salmon, where o'er river tides they rise. Then in brown autumn-time he seeks the scene Where the salt billows chafe the ocean shore, And from a rock engarlanded with weed.

Casts the long line where angry currents pour ; Takes the strip'd bass in his convulsive leaps. Or shapely bluefish swimming heedless by, Or weakfish glittering in the middle deeps, Or blackfish that in low abysSes lie.

In all these seasons of the rolling year,

The angler moves amid enchanting scenes, Where wreaths of flowers on bush and tree are

hupg,

Ivies and woodbines twine their bowery greens,Roses and lilies charm with rare perfume,

Great orchards droop with wealth of golden globes,

Daisies and clovers in the meadows bloom. And every floweret flaunts its color'd robes. Song birds salute him with the dawning light, The bobolink, robin and the minstrel thrush ; They chant their carols all the summer day,

While chirps the whippoorwill in evening hush ; All the blithe sights of Nature cheer his eyes, All Nature's voices charm with glad surprise.

REVISITING FISHING SCENES OF OLD.

When I revisited my childhood's stream

After long years, I saw a saddening change ;

The beech leaves still were imaged o'er its space. The grassy banks were verdant as of yore, The vine still hung its fox-grape cluster there, The bubbling joy of boblink, from its nest, Still to my ear came sweetly as of old ;

But the bright fish that glitter'd in the deeps, And all glad life that 'livened the green shores, Were sadly absent. Underneath the bridge. Where I so oft the silvery schools had watch'd, No fish were seen. Now on the briery fence The English sparrow had usurp'd Bob White ; The pond was all unwrinkled by a fin,

The turtles black that bask'd on mossy log Seem'd few and small, the water snakes had gone: The little crawfish shooting to and fro,

The eels, the hair worms and pollywogs,

That wriggled once in shallows and spring runs, The water beetles that in eddies whirl'd,

Seem'd to have vanish'd from *my* childhood haunt ; For lapsing years had wrought a wasteful change ! Oh! old delights! when bobbing for lithe eels In dusky nights! when shone the transient lamps Of luminous fireflies o'er the clouded wave. While from • the darkling dome above came cries

Of nighthawk and the mournful hoot of owl, The whistle of the woodcock in the glooms, The hollow drum of partridge in the wood ; Then in the shades the heron of the night, Robed in gray plumes, would settle by my side Yet other boon companionship was mine, When droning booms of bullfrog would arise And tinklings of the insect would resound.

The old millpond held treasures in those days, And chief the pickerel 'mid the lilypads;

Then, oh ! what joy to draw the meshing seine And gather in the precious wealth it held ! No string of trout hung by the campfire blaze Look'd e'er so grand as sucker and the chub, The catfish, sunfish and the slippery eels, And snapping turtles, that those meshes held. The millrace held rare wonders in those days, When dropped my fish line thro' the sawmill floor ; There seem'd no costlier fishes in the world Than those that sported in that sawdust pool!

RESORTS OF THE ANGLER.

The angler, ah ! what lovely scenes Surround him in his devious ways The poet
may but faintly sketch

Th' elysian haunts through which he strays . In vain the artist's mingled hues
Would paint the landscape that he views. 'Mid scenes of beauty lies his path,
Following the river's winding sweeps; He sees it in the rapid's dash,
In bold cascade he sees its leaps; He knows its silent. dusky depths,
Its shallows, pav'd with golden sand ; The bordering flowers delight his sense.
And sedges rustling o'er the strand. The lark and robin sing to him,
The bobolink and brown thrush trill ;

All feather'd tenants of the grove
His ear with mellow greetings fill. He seeks in some lone wilderness
Some lake that in calm beauty rests, Where oaks around its borders press. Waving
their leafy. plumy crests. And when red autumn stains the year, In princely
garments they uprear, Drooping above the limpid tide
Their flaunting banners, yellow-dyed ; As wardens old, their vigils keep To
guard an infant monarch's sleep.
Then, too, his way is by the sea, Along the rock-engirdled coast. Where the
curl'd billows leap in foam And surges o'er the rocks are tost, There, ever in the
summer's prime,
It is a pleasant haunt. I weep,
When ocean beats its whisper'd chime,
Soft murmuring in its sleep serene. Then winds are soft and waves are bright,
And beach sands sparkle in the light. And the smooth, rounded, crested waves
Roll in like turfy, rural graves.
And flocks of sea mews skim the deep Or high in airy circles sweep.
So here from some brown-weeded rock
His eye beholds the vast expanse ;
He views with awe that world of waves, Whirling and sparkling in their dance ;
Anon he casts the far-sent line
To drag the bluefish to their doom, Or drops his tackle in the deeps
For sea bass in abysmal gloom ; He sees the Spanish mackerel whirl In glittering
antics o'er the wave, Or in some salty channel takes
The mighty tarpon, swift and brave.

FLOWER-CROWNED FLORIDA.

'Mid thy fair realms, 0 flower-crowned Florida! The angler finds his paradise of sport ;

Soft airs around him waft perennial sweets.

And welcome him to each belov'd resort. The rare magnolias ope their flow'ry cones.

The orange groves for him exhale perfumes. Each leaf and orchid and each frill of fern

Thro' all the woodlands spread delicious blooms.

Here in the river deeps, the channel tides.

Hasten. 0 angler, with thy tackle fine : Here cast the luring fly, the mullet bait.

And rarest sport and rich reward be thine! There tarpon, silver king, leaps high in air, Yet seeks to break thy barbed hook in vain; In vain he plunges, dashes o'er the wave. Then yields. exhausted, to thy steady strain. Amid the mangrove isles the black drum bask, The swift crevalle glide by grassy shore ; The mangrove snapper lurks in abyss de-p,

The sheepshead feed where inlet salt-tides pour; In deep recesses of the winding creeks,

In salt lagoons of Indian River tide.

The groupers red, the gamest fish that swim, Pursuing helpless prey remorseless glide ; And here, 0 angler. thy supremest care Is taxed to drag the grouper from
his lair !

Amid this lovely land of havens. rivers, isles, An endless wealth of rarest fish are found ; The rich pompanos, silver fish and jew, Kingfish and rockfish everywhere abound; Fiercest of al(the sawfish and the shark

Skim the smooth wave or lurk in waters dark!

"The groves were God's first temples."
-BRYANT.

FLORIDA FISHING.

Here by the salt lagoons, the wild fowl's haunt; Where red flamingoes and the white swans sweep, Where the tall water oaks their branches droop. And green magnolias hem the currents deep ; Beneath the tufted groves that fringe the stream, Where lilies bloom and crimson roses gleam ; Here where the mangrove-isles, like emerald
gems,
The glassy surface of the seas inlay,
The angler comes with swinging rod and line To seek the pastimes of his holiday.
0 sumptuous region ! the Creator's hand
Has sown so prodigal with floral blooms. There is no paradise on earth so fair,
So rich with flowery charms and rare perfumes Here the great tarpon, armor'd with bright scales Like plated cuirass of the burnish'd steel. The swift cavalle and the channel bass
Dart thro' the deeps and o'er the eddies wheel.
By sandy beach or o'er the reedy marsh, Where curlews whistle and the plovers cry, For mangrove snapper and pompano rare
We cast the humming line and feather'd fly ; And lure the grouper from the cavern'd deeps, The spot and sea trout in their flashing leaps.
We love to tread the broad Savannah's space, The groves where oranges their
globes display Beneath whose vaulted roofs the
smilax twines. Hydrangeas lift the rosy-tinted spray, Dahlias and asters and the starry phlox
Blossom perennial in the tropic air ;
And all the colors that boon Nature loves
Enchanting bloom, luxuriant and fair.

THE CHANNEL BASS OF FLORIDA.

'<this mid-winter of the Northern Coast
I love to dream of semi-tropic clime.
Here rivers pulseless rest in death-like sleep.
And gleams the icicle and frosty rime.
Here naked woods are smother'd in the snow, The pastures buried in a gelid sheet.
An icy shroud envelopes the broad lake.
And Winter reigns in every lone retreat. Then 'tis a joy to muse on foreign realm.
Where lofty woodlands line each placid stream, Where sweet magnolias and the orange grove Bend with their fruits, with perfum'd blossoms
gleam.
There where o'er marsh, or by the shelly shore. The wild fowl skim on balanc'd wings the air, The fowler reaps the harvest of the game.
The anglers keen the abundant pastimes share. In sandy coves engirt with flowery blooms,
By trickling rivulets fring'd with marshy grass, Thro' surge and river glides the tarpon grand, And mid the mangrove isles swim channel bass. In spring-time swarm their numbers in the bay,
Flashing at inlets, in the flow of tide.
O'er the sand-flats and by the shores they range, Seeking their food as dashingly they glide, Pursuing mullet in their greedy race,

> And, shark-like, ravaging the salty flood—
> Remorseless tyrants of the watery space.

In the warm season of the summer time
The surf is redden'd by their gleaming sides. They glitter where the frothy billow breaks. They flash above the ripples of the tides. Fearless and frantic, round the fisher's boat
They plunge, they spring to seize the tempting
bait,
Fight to the death, surrender to their fate! More fierce in fight, more valiant in career, A fish impetuous is the tarpon grand.
Monarch of all the rangers of the Gulf.

Matchless in vigor by the salty strand!
The channel bass, so famed for strength and speed, May ill compare with tarpon's savage might. The bluefish and the shark ne'er rival him in fight, Yet the skilled angler, with his tackle fine, Triumphant meets this tiger of the brine.

TARPON FISHING IN FLORIDA.

The tarpon is the crowned king. The royal chief of tropic seas. No rover of the watery worlds May rival its sublimities ;

Supreme in mighty strength it roves In Mexic Gulf, Floridian coast. Swifter than shaft from Indian bow. A matchless, a resistless host !

Symmetric in his rounded form. With fins of ample size and sweep, Stern is its fight for liberty,

O'er the great billows of the deep, For on its armor'd back is set A sharpen'd, dangerous bayonet !

Who may describe those plated scales Of burnished steel, of silver hue ? Smooth as a shaft of iron,

Clear as a crystal drop of dew,

They glisten like the moon's white beam When high the victim leaps in air, Rising like a sunset gleam,

Struggling and raging in despair—Six feet of valor mad with strife,

Two hundred weight of desperate life ! The bait is cast—the mullet bait ; It sinks, it slowly sinks from sight, But sudden—swift it onward moves ;

Now angler strike, and strike with might ! Now, now begins strategetic war, Free liberty, dark death the stake!

With dexterous ruse. with brave assault, Striving the tackle strong to break. The victim caught by fatal lure, Stung by the sharp, deep-planted steel, Plunges amain, then leaps in air. While hums the swift-revolving reel : At last—and after hours of strife, Of anxious toil o'er briny fields. The silver monarch parts with life. And to the cruel gaff-hook yields ! The sportman's eager thirst for game The countless bison herds have slain, Exterminated the elephant From Africa's barbaric plain, In Asiatic jungles swept

Tiger and lion from their haunt But in these seas the silver king

With man and shark may long contend, But at the last, the battle o'er Those kings extinct, will reach the end

" You see the ways the fisherman doth take

To catch the fish ; what engines doth he make? Behold ! how he engageth all his wits ;

Also his snares, lines, angles, hooks and nets ; Yet fish there he that neither hook nor line, Nor snare, nor net, nor engine can make thine ; They must be groped for, and be tickled, too, Or they will not be catched, whate're you do."
- BUNYAN.

MENHADEN.

O'er ocean waters, sound and bay
The twinkling June-time sunbeams play ; And white with foam the billows shine
Where the mossbunkers lash the brine Above them flocks of seagulls swing ;
Beneath, the hungry bluefish spring. And deadlier still the surfmen strain
The oar, and run the meshing seine.
Where sweeps the broad and breezy bay Engirt by shores and woodlands gay, In shoals innumerable as sands
That sparkle o'er the wrinkled strands The bunkers gather on the flood,
Roaming the ocean paths for food ; And here the fisher-boats invade,
Deep with the shining burden weigh'd.
Off by the low New Jersey shore, Off where Long Island's surges roar, Off where the Narragansett Bay Its tribute to the sea doth pay, Off Massachusetts Bay profound,
Off Maine shores with their pinewoods crown'd, Off where the billows chafe and fret O'er rocks along New Brunswick set, These fish innumerable pass O'er stormy seas, o'er seas of glass.

" The water is the eldest daughter of the creation, the element upon which the Spirit of God did first move."
-IZAAK WALTON.

BLUEFISH.

Far as the foamy billows sweep, From northern reef to Arctic pole,
Far over islands of the deep,
Where tides incessant roll,
The bluefish, roamers of the seas.
Their endless voyagings urge ; Now plunging low in salt abyss.
Now leaping o'er the surge.
Where lovely shores of Florida,
Enamel with their blooms,
The broad Savannah and the coves,
Delicious with perfumes,
There rove the mangrove snapper schools.
The tarpon, "silver king,"
The pompano, the bright cavalle,
Then fierce thro' salt tides spring
The bluefish in their sudden leap, The tyrants of the deep !
They swarm along each rocky coast.
By Hatteras capes they glide ; Where Barnegat its inlet opes
To greet the swelling tide, In salty cove, in breezy bay,
In channel tides and sound. Their gleaming multitudes abound.
      Greedy for finny prey.
      Shapely are they, like pirate craft
Remorseless to assail,
Fair with their rounded, graceful sides,
And the sharp, fork'd tail.
The angler from some jutting reef
Casts out his spinning line
The fleet-wing'd, dashing yachts pursue
The bluefish o'er the brine,
And cruel pound and meshing seine Ensnare these rovers of the main.

BOSTON MACKEREL.

Far o'er the seas, bright rovers of the deep, From Tropic to Equator range your shoals, From Belle Isle Strait to St. Helena's Isle, Far as the surges break, the billow rolls,

Far up the Bosphorus and Marmara's sea,

Your starry fins glide thro' the circling seines, While in their light cazieques the swarthy crews Pursue, rewarded oft with sumptuous gains;

And there great cormorants gather from the skies And with their greedy beaks dispute the prize. Near all the rounded year on Irish coast

Your rainbow legions swarm along the deep,

From cliff and beach the fishers watch your shoals, And quick their gallant shallops round ye sweep. Up the St. Lawrence, far as eye may range, The clamoring gulls and puffins mark your way ; They swoop, they revel in the dainty fare,

And to pursuing boats your route betray:

Round green New England coasts your numbers swarm,

They sweep past rocky cliffs and reefs of Maine. In Massachusetts Bay. from cape to cape.

Your shining columns lash the watery plain.

Oft by Brant Rock, off Marshfield's famous shore. Or Point of Manumet in
Plymouth Bay,

My little boat. fast anchor'd. far from land, Among thy shoals has gained the ample prey.. Those gleaming, leaping, rapid shoals, entice The hardy fishers all along the coast ;

On the Grand Banks of Newfoundland they swarm, Roaming in myriad schools, a countless host ;

And here, in storm and calm. the mustering fleet Ravage the shoals in their deep-sea retreat.

COD. HADDOCK AND HALIBUT.

In the Bay of Chaleur
And afar where the Bank Of Newfoundland stretches
So foggy and dank;
In their black little schooners
The fishermen sail.
Now cradled in calm,
Now tossed in the gale, For weeks and for months
O'er those dangerous shoals Adrift on the ocean,
The fishing-fleet rolls.
Yet undaunted the crews,
Though life be at stake, Cast hook for the halibut,
Haddock and hake;
They dash o'er the seas.
While canvas will draw,
Though the gusts blow in tempests,
Or subside in light flaw.

In past years I've had rare fishing day Beyond the islands that gem the wave. Far off o'er shoals of Middle Bank, In Massachusetts' breezy bay:

Ne'er anchoring our schooner trim, Drifting all night with lanterns lit, But when the dawn illum'd the East. And shadows of the night would flit. Then all around would dart and flash The Boston mackerel with a dash. And soon our deck with scaly spoil, The treasures of our angling toil, Would glitter, and that tempting bait Would lure the haddock to their fate, And twenty fathoms deep would take The codfish, halibut and hake.

DRUMFISH *(Pogonias Chromis).*

The rolling drum, the muffled drum That summons men to arms,
That sounds from fort and battlement The reveille's alarms,
That in the cities and in camp
Rolls out its stirring note.
Sounding o'er land and over seas, Wherever banners float,
Yet here beneath the rippling tides
It yields a hoarse and smothered sound, Where the salt current glides,
Is a hollow-murmured hum
Showing the presence of the drum. It is the bulkiest of fish,
The angler takes with rod and line Found o'er all regions of the coast, Haunting the ocean brine ;
Its Winter home is where the woods Of Florida are green,
Feeding where Sheepshead fish abide, On mollusks of the tide,
But when Midsummer's skies are bright.
They leave their southern home, Ranging the broad New Jersey coast
Reveling in the foam ;
The fisher's seine enmeshes them As they rush swimming past,
But anglers standing by the surf Their circling hand lines cast.
And soon the monstrous fish are caught And struggling to the shore are brought.
The black drum is a mighty fish, Heavy and strong of fin.
Armor'd with large symmetric scales. A victim hard to win
His jaw is lined with sounded teet:„ Crushing the mussel-shell.
Grinding the hard clam in its crust Or oyster in its cell,
So strong and gamesome that it tries The anglers prowess till it dies.

BLACKFISH, OR TAUTOC.

I love to muse o'er rocks that throw Their shadows on the tides below, And note the varied life that sweeps The salt abysses of the deeps.

The blue-fish, leaping as they pass,

The brown-strip'd, pearl-enamell'd bass. The crab, the shrimp, the mussel-shell. The sea-egg, with its thorny cell, The moss to slippery rock that clings. The kelp. the seaweed with its rings, The lavish treasures of the sea. Forever precious unto me.

Here, where the salt-tides ebb and flow Over the brown rocks, deep below, The greedy blackfish come to share The shelly bounties ever there ; Then rod is swung, and whistling line Draws out the victims from the brine.

WEAKFISH.

Now in these latest days of May The boats are out in breezy bay, Fast by some point that juts its bar. Its rocky buttresses deep and far ; Or by some river mouth that pours Its affluent current by the shores, The fisher casts his baited line, To tempt the weakfish of the brine.

Long Island! where thy bays extend. Or where thy ocean borders trend, What joyous pastime thou dost yield To angler o'er thy watery field I

Ah, bright my golden days have sped. Where Barnegat's salt billows spread, Many the blissful hours I knew Amid Virginian waters blue.

When from the pastures of the deep The finny harvests I would reap.

SEA BASS FISHING.

It is a fair September day, yet skies are overcast. Scarce ripple on the wave, scarce whisper in the blast ;

The tides are flowing in.

By Gardiner's Island

shore

O'er sunken rock and pebbly reef tumultuous they pour.

Where barnacles and shell-fish are plenteous in the tides

The sea-bass gather to the feast that nature kind provides.

So, 'tis a day for rod and hook and for the angler's line

Then cast the baited steel, where boils the sparkling brine.

O'er some gray, granite ledge, that hems the andy land

Equip'd with pliant rod. he hopeful takes his stand, With skillful hand he casts afar, his choice, enticing bait

To tempt the speckled-bass or sea-bass to their fate.

The plummet drops—the bait of clam or fiddler-crab sinks down

Prone where abyssmal deeps, with rocks are thickly sown,

Nor long he waits, for soon a jerk, a thrilling jerk is there,

The reel revolves, and quick a fish ascends to upper air.

A fisher with the hand-line is anchor'd in his skiff.

Far out where runs a reef from a projecting cliff ; A ripple blurs the surface that else were crystal-clear.

So. 'tis a day for royal sport—a day to angler dear.

The weak-fish glitter past, the blue-fish flash around.

Yet he seeks for other game, that swim in depths profound.

He fishes where the sea-bass or speckled bass resort

For to lure these noble fish is his supremest sport.

THE VETERAN SPORTSMAN.

The veteran sportsman! wide the natural world Hath welcomed him, all perfect joys to share. Hath welcomed him, each dawning light to greet. Or taste the sweetness of the evening air

Hath lured him forth from busy life's turmoil, From sordid search for luxuries and wealth,

To breathe the mountain airs. the ocean breeze. Invigorating heart and limb with health ;

The scenes, the sports. the pastimes of old days Bloom in the garden of his memories,

When on his brow Age drops its silvery crown. And life's long road behind him faded lies. In fancy's dream, in memory's magic glass, Still bloom perennial each familiar scene: The groves of childhood still as lovely stretch,

The pastures and the meads still spread as green. The twisting brook that prattled down the vale Still sings to him the melodies of old,

Chanting to him the same blithe madrigals. As it runs races o'er its sands of gold.

The wilding flowers enamel still the plain, Lavish with perfume blow the breezes sweet, The song birds yet their operas rehearse,

And with wild symphonies the veteran greet. The tufted groves bid welcome to their shades. The quail flock flutters o'er the stubbles still.

The partridge drums, the snipe skims o'er the
marsh,

The upland plover circles o'er the hill:

All sights and sounds, familiar in the past,

Still cheer his heart while life and memory last. He well remembers old October times,

Follows again the bevies of the quail.

Or by each tussock-haunt and brambly hedge He drops the snipe and woodcock as they sail.

By shaded stream that through the woodland
twines,

He marks the wood-duck and the blue-winged teal; O'er breezy bay or far extending marsh,

He sees the mallard and the widgeon wheel.

In those past years no cares disturbed his mind. Their perfect bliss in memory is enshrined! Kind ever in the pastimes of the field. He hath no frets, he ne'er triumphant boasts: He yields fair precedence in game resorts, O'er upland spaces, or by ocean coasts. In field, in forest, 'tis his honest aim, To warn the poacher and protect the game;

For each young sportsman he hath gracious mood. Teaching him lessons of the bay and wood; Perfect in health and joyous in his ways, He cheers with sunny speech inclement days: Hath ever kindliest word and helping hand, A cheerful nature to dispel life's gloom, And so his name and memory will survive On earth, while resting in the tomb!

THE SPORTSMAN'S GREETING.

Come, brother sportsmen, loving well the joys of rod and gun,
Come, for the field-sport season its glorious term hath run;
Hang up the fav'rite fowling-piece and cartridge belt on wall,
And by the social fire-side past ecstacies recall, And in these thrilling pages review each joyous scene
Recorded for your pleasure in Wildwood's Magazine.
Come, brethren of the rod dear anglers who have pass'd
Each season by the waters, with many a skilful cast,
Have followed thro' o'erhanging woods, the trout-stream on its way,
And by the surging ocean have gathered finny prey ;
Now lay aside the pliant rod, forsake the lake serene,

And here renew the joys of yore in Wildwood's Magazine.
Come, tourists who have wandered o'er hills and prairies wide,
Enjoying nature's wonders by woods and ocean tide,
Have climbed the soaring cliffs and scal'd the dizzy mount,
Have trod the flowery vales and bath'd in crystal fount.
Now put aside the tourist's staff, again enjoy each scene,
Depicted in the pages of Wildwood's Magazine. Come, winsome maid and matron, who oft explor'd the woods,
And visited in hunter's camp, by forest and by floods,
Have gathered blooms, have grac'd the board, and cast the silken line,
Have dreamed beneath the branches of hemlock and of pine,
Re-visit in soft fancies the wilds where you have been,
Pen-pictured in the columns of Wildwood's Magazine.
When spring-time spreads its em'rald green. boon Nature's forest bloom
The spicy breath of woodlands, the verdure, the perfume ;
Dear sportsman, think of pastimes by forest and by plain,
The glorious sport o'er prairies, and by the sounding main ;
Good angler. cast in fancy's spell the humming line once more,
Brave tourist, yet again the secret wilds explore ; Fair maiden, as you muse within the lighted hall, Those transports of the wilderness in memory
recall,
Those happy days, and blissful joys in each enchanting scene,
Again revealed in glowing lines of Wildwood's Magazine.   97

THE SPORTSMAN'S LOVE OF NATURE.

Good sportsman, thou hast ever lov'd to trace The streams, the woods of nature's vast domain, Loving to wander in the forest depths, Loving to meditate o'er grassy plain. Far in thy kingdoms. Nature, it is sweet, To tread thy precints wheresoe'er they be, Whether in flowery gardens of the land Or mountain fastnesses supremely grand. The hunters and explorers love to climb The craggy boulders, the granitic steep Where in dark caverns lurks the grizzly bear, The homes of bighorn, the great mountain sheep. With daring step he treads the wild ravine, The stony gulch, the canon's wide expanse, Where beetling precipices bar the way, Shunning no perils in his hold advance. Boon Nature with allurements charms the mind, By woods and waters, wildernesses green. Where leafy bowers endrape the tufted groves, Where verdurous slopes and valleys intervene. In the far south where orange orchards spread And waves are gemm'd by many a mangrove isle, Where twisting vines their garlands interweave, And flowery blooms in all the regions smile, There o'er the limpid surface swarm the fish, The giant tarpon cleaves the salty brine, The channel bass and sheepshead lurk in deeps. And swift cavalles and pompanos shine There is sumptuous pastime for his art, With rod and line so dear to angler's heart. He loves to saunter by the ocean shore. To mark the boiling surfs, the yeasty foam, To view the rippling billows as they flash, The crested breakers o'er the surface comb ; 'Tis there in boat he skims across the wave, Casts line for bluefish or the sable bass, For Spanish mackerel or the bright squeteague. In waters rough. or limpid— clear as glass. In Nature's realms, by seaside or by woods He loves her well in all capricious moods.

THE SPORTSMAN'S CARNIVAL SEASON.

Welcome autumnal sports, autumnal scenes, Welcome the rambles in autumnal groves.
Fair scenes, sweet sounds—bird songs in ever-
greens,
The woodcocks' flight. the cooing of wood doves. The squirrels' chatter in the hickory tree,
The plovers' whistle o'er the upland space The cries of baybirds by the shores of sea,
The whirl of wild fowl in erratic race,
The honk of wild geese o'er the waters' face. Enchantress Nature, with her magic wand, Fills with rare wonders the autumnal land ; The orchards bend with golden fruitage then,
The harvest fields are opulent with grain, The woods wave gorgeous banners in the glen, Wheat shocks spread tents o'er cultivated plain. The pasture oaks wear a gilded crown,
The elm trees lift their oriflamme of brown. The maple's foliage blushes with a stain. Far in the wild west rove the antler'd deer. The nimble antelopes circle in career ;
O'er the wide grain fields and where corn is ripe, The speckled grouse flocks on quick pinions sail,
O'er the oozy marshes flit the shy jack-snipe,
O'er shaded stream skim wood duck and the teal,
While o'er the tussock grasses of the vale
The startled bevies of the whistling quail
In coverts hide, or o'er the stubbles wheel. We love to hear the fowler's gun resound.
The sheep bells' tinkle and the low of herds. All tones of rural life, wherever found :
The hum of insects and the songs of birds,
The locust's drone, the whip-poor-will's lament,
The swallow's chirp, the murmur of the bee. The squirrel's chatter in his leafy tent,
The echoing cheer of children full of glee,
O'er sunny slope at play, or dancing round the tree.

Then comes the angler with his rod and reel, In anchored skiff he haunts the glassy lake, Intent to watch the shining victims break ; Or seeks the sandy borders of the shore, Where the salt billows of the ocean pour, There with lithe rod the bluefish prize to take.

SPORTSMEN'S CLUBS.
These are not soldiers. arm'd. equipp'd for war, Marching in ranks with gun and flashing sword. The fires of battle blazing in their eye,
Charging some fort where blood is lavish pour'd; Yet they are valiant and athletic all,
Skillful with weapon and inur'd to toil,
Prompt with their lives should e'er their country call.
These are not seamen, sailing the broad seas, Braving the terrors of the raging main. Manning the guns of great embattled fleets. Dauntless in storm or battle's hurricane ;
Yet in their shapely yachts these rule supreme. Triumphant ever where strange barks compete : Fearless and cool when thrashing thro' the seas. When fierce tornadoes 'gainst the canvas beat.
They are a kindly fellowship of men,
Of genial soul, of generous, liberal hand, Who love in unison to share the joys,
The manly sports of ocean or of land.
They love when first the dusky dome of sky
Is tin g'd with pearly light and crimson hues, O'er dew-wet grass to seek the shaded stream, Soon as the shimmering beams the waves suf-
fuse,
Or when the sunset leaves a glorious trail,
A splendor more of heaven than earthly vale ; For then and there they know the spangled trout Seeking their prey athwart the surface swim, Eager to banquet on the insect tribes,

HAUNTS OF WILD GAME.

Whose glittering wings the crystal surface skim; And there the angler's feather'd fatal lure

Drops softly down the victim to secure.

So, tob, by ocean surf or salty bay

They skim in shapely yacht the foaming deep. There take the Spanish mackerel. rich with dyes. Or ravenous bluefish as they upward leap. Anchor'd by rocky reef or shelly bar

They cast the baited hook for sable bass, Or up St. Lawrence swing the skillful rod

To take the springing salmon as they pass. So, too, the social sportsmen seek the plain, The prairie realm immeasurably spread.

Where tassell'd corn-fields stretch, and golden

grain,

And the grouse-flocks with liberal feasts are fed ; O'er stubble-fields they track the whistling quail. Or the shy woodcock at the rivulet edge, Or drop the fluttering baybirds on the wing. Or where they settle by the yellow sedge.

But nobler still their sport. their perfect joy. When hid in ambush'd boat at breezy bay, O'er mid the reedy marshes of the shore,

They watch the geese-flocks pass in long array, Or mark the brant in dense platoons sweep past. The canvasbacks and redheads sweeping by, The blackduck legions speeding far and fast,

The   swift-wing'd sprigtail and the mallard shy ; Then great the joy and glorious the prize

As each new victim falls to earth and dies.

" Oh ! who that hath an eye to see, A heart to feel, a tongue to bless, Can ever undelighted be

WIth Nature's loveliness ?"

-UNKNOWN AUTHOR.

61

NATIONAL SPORTSMEN'S ASSOCIATION.

Come, brother sportsmen loving well the pastimes of the field,

The joys of rod and gun, the woods and waters yield ;

Come with united voice the wisest laws to frame, That shall protect from slaughter the fishes and the game.

Come from the Union States a patriotic band, That shall protect the game through all our native land.

Come brethren of the roddear anglers who have pass'd

Each season by the waters, with many a skillful cast,

Have follow'd thro' o'er branching woods, the trout stream on its way,

And by the surging ocean have gather'd finny prey ;

Come tourists who have roamed o'er hills and prairies wide

Enjoying Nature's wonders by stream and ocean tide,

Have climbed the soaring cliffs, and scaled the craggy mount,

Have trod the flowery dale, and bath'd in crystal fount ;

Now meet in this White City, rehearsing pleasures past,

Suggesting laws protective that shall forever last. When Nature opes its treasure, its beauty and its bloom,

The spicy breath of woodlands, the verdure and perfume,

Dear sportsmen think of past times o'er forest and o'er plain,

The glorious sports of prairies, the joys by salty main;

Good angler cast in fancy the humming line once more,

Brave tourist once again the bowery wilds explore. Fair maiden as you muse within this lighted hall The transports of the wilderness in memory recall. The jocund days, the blissful joys in each enchant-
ing scene.
Beside the rippling waters, beneath the forests green.
True sportsmen ever are a brave, chivalric race. Obedient to the laws of angling and the chase, Ever a gracious fellowship, a fond fraternal band Of kindly souls, of generous deeds and open hand ; Who love in unison to share the sport
Of waters' realm and Nature's court.

"Truly this life is precious to the root,
And good the feel of grass beneath the foot ;
To lie in buttercups and clover bloom,
Tenant in common with the bees,
And watch the white clouds drift through gulfs of trees, Is better than long waiting
in the tomb."
-UNKNOWN AUTHOR.

AUDUBON'S MONUMENT.

Ah, noble Audubon, who lov'd so well
Thro' Nature's loveliest. loneliest woods to tread, To paint with matchless brush
and loving heart. The birds of song thro' her dominions spread ; To track with
patient toil the forest glades, A wanderer lone in wildernesses drear.
Toiling o'er Northern mount and Southern plain, Unwearied with thy task thro'
all the year. Dear to us all is thy illustrious fame, Deep in our hearts we
consecrate thy name!
'Mid solemn silence or the sylvan sounds Of woods primeval, thou did'st love
to rove, Noting all bird-life of those leafy shades. Rejoicing in their joys, their
songs of love, The birds that skimm'd the empty fields of air. The birds that thro'
the sombre forests sped, The flocks that o'er the boundless prairies flew, The sea-
fowl o'er the salty lagoons spread, Were all familiar in each tone and hue;
Each gorgeous plumage, each melodious note. Each hovering wing that o'er your
head would float ;
Sweet then the task the master's hand to trace Each grace, each glory of the
feathered race !
Then let us raise a fair, memorial shaft, Sculptur'd with birds of every race and
clime, Grac'd with thy lineaments, thy honor'd name, Memorial of our love thro'
future time. Let it arise where first the glow of day Around its shapely
pinnacle may fall. And sunset's rosy colors
shall suffuse The graven name so precious to us
all.
There then the birds you lov'd their songs shall
pour,
Delicious harmonies of wood and vale, Where royal eagle shall above ye soar
And evening whippoorwill sound mournful wail.

FRANK FORESTER'S MONUMENT.

Come. brethren, consecrate the shrine, The fluted shaft or marble urn,

O'er which morn's earliest beam may shine, And twilight's latest incense burn ; A fair memorial on whose face Thy name, dear Herbert. we may trace.

Place not the shaft in cloister'd aisle. Where never blessed light may smile, Not in Cathedral grim and gray,

Where brightening daylight ne'er may stray. 'Mid charnel stones and ancient mold, And tatter'd fringe of canker'd gold ; But rather place it on some height, When free the breezes sweep their flight, Where blaze of sun or moonbeam blest, Or gleam of star may on it rest; So that the pilgrim wandering there, May gaze entranced on landscape fair. On purpled hills, on tufted grove, Where Herbert's footstep lov'd to rove, On grassy plain and flowing stream, On Greenwood lake, with all its gleam, O'er upland pasture, bowery grot, That once had echoed to his shot. Gaze down, see crystal streamlets shine, Where he had cast the angler's line; The lake engirdled with its wood. Where he the fisher's art pursued ; Where far away, and fair to view To the horizon's hazy blue,

The Warwick woodlands gloriously Roll their brown billows like a sea. Lover of nature I his delight To watch the constellations bright, To see the glory of the day,

Shine over mount or prairies gay. To see the woods majestic spread Their glooms, their wildernesses dread. And follow to their inmost heart,

The joys so dear to sportsman's heart. Here will the fluttering songbirds sing. Their tuneful madrigals of spring. The purple dove her plaint will pour, The meadow-lark will upward soar, The whippoorwill when eve is dim, Will chant her sorrowful. sweet hymn, While from the thicket of the vale. Pipeth the shrill responsive quail, And all the sights and sounas of love, Will consecrate the dusky grove.

LINES TO A BROTHER SPORSTMAN.

To my cousin, SAMUEL. C. CLARKE, (aged yz years), author of "Flailing in Florida," and elder brother of the late Rev. JAMES FRP EMAN CLARKE.

Yes! here where once we used to swim. And where our sailboats used to skim, And where our holidays were pass'd, And baited hooks and lines were cast, Where golden hours and youthful joys Were all too short for us. gay boys, Rise stately roofs and palaces,

Embower'd 'mid flowers and drooping trees: Where crowded streets and noble squares. The city's crowded thoroughfares, And fashion's pomp. and busy trade. And gentle lover's promenade,

Have long usurped the watery space, And left of our old haunts no trace ! Of all those schoolmates few remain, Few links of the long-sunder'd chain : Few of that group that loved to pass O'er the old Common's sacred grass, Or gather where the old Elm stood, The latest patriarch of the wood

Who down the Beacon slope would ride On snow sled, or with swift skates glide Who lo•'d in summer afternoon,

When leaves were green and birds in tune. To gather where the Rope-Walk gave

Its welcome to the tidal wave,
Just where the Public Garden now
Spreads flowery blooms and leafy bough!
A marvellous, vast change, I ween,
Is there where those old joys have been Those days I love now to recall—The days of cricket, bat and ball, The days of marbles, tops and kite, So brimm'd with pleasure and delight! The days of fishing sport. so dear,
At Cambridge Bridge or Long Wharf pier ; The days of bliss, when life was new, When joys were many, cares so few !
Few of that bright, rejoicing train, In all the walks of life remain ; And in that few I haply meet,
On stately square or crowded street, I see no long-familiar trace
In snowy hair and wrinkled face! The limbs that used to run like deer, Are crippled in life's long career ; The hands once skilled to pull the oar Or swing the rod are strong no more. Some sleep in dust of native land, And some repose on foreign strand; Some by the palm trees of the shore. Where Indian billows rave and roar ; Some where Pacific billOws sweep,
Long since have laid them down to sleep; And some are reverend preachers now, Of solemn step and thoughtful brow, Or merchant princes, rich in gold, The playmates of those days of old ; But all are mindful of the joys Of that far time when they were boys!

DEDICATORY TO - FIELD AND STREAM."

This whole region, spreading far and wide, Thrills with its beauties every human soul, Its spacious grassy plains, its craggy mounts, The limpid streams that thro' its spaces roll, Entrance and fascinate each sportsman's heart, And to his senses ardent joys impart.

It is the purpose of this journal new

To sketch the features of this lovely land,

To lead the readers thro' those magic realms. The hills, the plains that charm on every hand ; The countless lakes, so fair, so picturesque, Where the glad angler finds sumpreme delight ; The sparkling brooks, the rivers broad and deep That pour thro' shaded groves, or flash with light ! We guide the hunter o'er our beetling cliff, We lead his step thro' gulch and canyon wild Where range the deer, elk, moose and antelope That have for ages thro' those haunts defiled Good Sportsman I Thou hast ever lov'd to trace The streams, the woods of Nature's vast domain, Loving to ramble in the forest-depths.

Loving to meditate o'er grassy plain ;

Far in thy kingdoms, Nature, it is sweet To tread thy precints, wheresoe'er they be. Whether in flowery gardens of the land, Or mountain fastnesses supremely grand! The hunters and explorers love to climb The craggy boulders, and the granite steep, Where in grim cavern lurks the grizzly bear

The homes of big-horn, the bold mountain sheep ;

With daring step he treads the wild ravine,

The dusky chasm with its vast expanse, Where rugged precipices bar the way,

Shunning no perils in his brave advance !

WITH RIFLE AND SHOT GUN.

THE GUN.

In Autumn-time, when pearly dews are glistening on the grass,
And the crimsons of the dawnings enkindle clouds of air,
And every passing breeze adds elixer to the blood. Then Nature bids the sportsmen to woods and wilds repair.

In long-departed years our favorite shooting gun Was the muzzle-loading piece, reliable and true ; It was a trusty weapon, forever in my hand In forest-land or thicket, or by the waters blue.

When the herbage of the prairies was touched with blighting frosts
And all harvests of the wheat-fields in graneries were bestowed,
And the shocks of golden corn, like tents, o'er-spread the field,
Then forth o'er stubble furrows exultingly I strode.

No other gun in those old days was known to sportsman's hand;
That flint-lock fowling-piece, so killing in the chase ;
Long ere percussion-caps their quick precision gave ;
Long ere the smart breech-loader usurped the old gun's place.
Yet with those arms now obsolete full many a joy I knew
When wild-geese flocks were passing, in wedge-shaped columns long,
When o'er the broad salt marshes the wildfowl flew in clouds
        The black duck and the widgeon, a migratory throng.
        When in the wood the partridge swept through the fir
and pine.
•

When in the tangled swamp the woodcock made its lair,
When from the stubble-tussocks swept bevies of the quail.
When by the salty shores the snipe-flocks skimmed the air.
But now the smart breech-loader is peerless in the field,
It reaches full perfection in shooting and in shape:
Such are the arms of Parker, Lancaster and Scott. Of Francotte and Forehand, whose
names be ne'er forgot,
Of American and the Ithaca, from which few birds escape.
With these our noble sportsmen are well equipt for fray,
In forests where the wild deer speep through the leafy glooms,
In upland pastures, where the flocks of plover skim the air,
Or where the snipe and wildfowl exult on rapid plumes.
Good brethren of the gun. who love the sports of field.
Be ever prompt and vigilant for game law rights to care,
Protecting in *close-time* the game of wave and wood,
The red deer of the woodlands, the birds that beat the air.

"One impulse from a vernal wood
May teach you more of man,
Of moral evil and of good
Than all the sages can."
-WORDSWORTH.

AUTUMN SPORT.

The greenwood shadows, grim and weird. Lie heavy in the forest shade :
But here and there the transient gleams
Fall brightly, and the woods prevade. There, in dense canopy of leaves,
Those beams illuminate with glow The verdant billows of the grass
That spread a sloping floor below. 'Tis a fair haunt, a lovely scene,
With tufted woods and opening stream—A sparkling brook that riotous
Slips o'er the sands with sudden gleam.
So here, in tussocks of the swamp. The lonely woodcock has its home.
Springing alarmed when sportsman's gun
Resoundeth in the thicket's gloom.
In tangled recess of the wood,
Where thick the pint trees weave a shade. The partridge rears her callow brood,
Those timid tenants of the glade.
'Midst golden grain, in stubble field.
The grouse flocks have secure retreat. Luxuriating in the fare
The bearded oats, the yellow wheat. And here the russet-plumag'd quail
Riots amid abundant feed,
Lurking amid the sheltering grass,
Or fleeing swift with frighten'd speed.
In   wildernesses of dense groves
Range   far   and free the dappled deer, Browsing beneath the dusky shades,
Or fleeing far in swift career—For here the hunter's deadly aim
Slaughters the wild, unwary game. O'er reedy marsh, o'er meadows salt.
The snipe-flocks in vast legions pour, Winging across the ample bays
Or o'er the beaches of the shore.

Here gray-wing'd willets speed their way. The sickle-bill curlew has flight,
The brant birds and the robin-snipe
Wheel high in air or prone alight. So, later yet, the sea-fowl flocks
The mallard and the pied-shell drake. The broad-bill and the brilliant teal-
Oler marsh and waves their journeys take. And by the sands and rocks of shore,
The migratory flocks of coot.
Of old-squaws, sea-ducks and the loon
Swing high in air beyond pursuit.
Thus endless pastimes and rare sport
Tempt gunners to each good resort.

WOODCOCK SHOOTING.

In August and September time, The season's rare, imperial prime, The ardent sportsman hies with gun To swampy clump or brooklet run,

For there where densest shades pervade The hidden haunt and thicket glade, The woodcocks lurk in hermit lair. Feeding at will on daintiest fare: So there, despite the toil and heat, The gunner seeks that dim retreat.

In Springtime they leave Southern ground For distant Northern regions bound, So when the early bluebirds sing In orchards of the budding Spring, And when their lays the robins chant The woodcocks migrate to their haunt. For snows have melted and the rains Have moistened all the loamy plains, And here in sheltered lowland space They find secluded feeding place ; And later, 'mid the alder woods. In bottom lands they rear their broods. Though lovers of low fens and swamps.

They ofttimes make their chosen camps In high spots. where no rains molest Their callow broods, secure in rest.

In warm Spring evenings one may hear The woodcock's whistle, loud and clear, His love notes soft as liquid strain Of rival songsters of the plain ;

With guttural prelude to his song He rises on his pinions strong,

In spiral circlings, high in flight,

His notes still heard, though lost to sight ; But sweeter still his liquid notes,

As downward to his nest he floats. Oft when afar is feeding ground From covert-haunt, they may be found Uprising, spirit-like, from glooms Of the dense woods, on dusky plumes ; Swift darting through the twilight skies, Thence to low bogs and brook he flies.

To angler, in the Summer's flush, Following the trout-brook's dashing rush, They oft their russet plumes display An instant, as they speed away,

Then in the thicket's densest screen Evanishing, no more are seen.

When Summer days are on the wane

And green leaves change to brighter stain, When crops are in and grass again Springs fresh along the harvest plain, Then the blithe bird hath swift career, Its whir of wing more sharp and clear.

THE RUFFED GROUSE, *(Bonasi Umbellus)*.

A score of intervening years

Hath vanished since 1 trod the scene Of early sports and wildwood joys, Yet still they bloom. forever green. In memory I recall each morn

That wood me, with the dawning light. Enticing me to meadow side,

O'er dewey grasses, twinkling bright And, as I paced the valleys wide,

The earliest songbirds tun'd their lay. The robin pour'd its soul of song. The blackbird trill'd on leafy spray. Then to the bosky groves I pass'd, To wilderness of solemn shade. Where pine and hemlock wove a screen,

And silence did pervade.

'Twas there where woodbines drap'd the oak,

And swinging grape vines intertwined.

Where mountain ash wore verdant crown.

And high in air soar'd plumy pine. That the shy partridge led its brood In dim recesses of the wood.

I lov'd to hear its rolling drum

Sound from some bole of fallen tree, Or startled, on affrighted wing.

Speed thro' the forests, far and free.

So dense the shade, that scarce a beam

Of light would gild the mossy floor, Where the pine-needles and the leaf

Had spread a russet carpet o'er,

Where scarce the gunner's step was heard To startle the unconscious bird.

When drifting snows o'erspread the ground,

They seek low roosts on thick-top'd tree, Or shelter'd spot where bushy-heap

Form'd covert in security ;

And there, on winter green and seed, In season of the winter feed.

They love a broad and breezy height.

A lofty ridge with woodlands crown'd.
Where flows a crystal mountain brook,
'Mid solitude of glooms profound.
There, o'er the tufted groves they sweep. Or over sunny slopes of green,
Gleaming a rich, delicious sheen. When Autumn feasts enrich the scene:
And then the hunter's zealous toil
Is crown'd with opulence of spoil.

JACK-SNIPE SHOOTING.

No birds so wild, erratic in their flight
As these wing'd rovers of the air and seas, Each fickle, sudden change of temperature, Each quick, capricious shifting of the breeze, Is follow'd by mutations in their flight. Hovering, hesitating. where they may alight. They restless change their favorite feeding-ground. Where they had revel'd in abundant feast, And causeless flit to other far resort,

Thus baffling well the shooter's toilful quest, So cheated sniper in its wonted haunt Oft fails to find the roving emigrant.

The golden rule for all who seek their flocks Is soft approach and silence most profound No bird so shy, no bird so keen of sense, To fly alarm'd at every faintest sound. O glorious Autumn I there is joy supreme In all thy rosy dawns
and purpled eves,

A charm by sparkling brook and river-stream,

In drooping woods with all their fluttering leaves. 'Tis then, o'er salty marsh and meadow-space We note the zig-zag flitting of the bird,

Hear its sharp "scaipe, scaipe" in the devious race, As o'er its grassy feeding-ground it whirrs. In Spring the meadows are not sole resort, Then oft they seek the upland pastures wide, Wet spots in fields of Winter wheat and rye,

Or grassy tussocks by the ditch's side ;

In windy weather they seek woodlands wet, Shelter'd by alders or a willow-hedge. Or spots on open marshes fenc'd around With bending rushes, or the yellow sedge, Though oft they migrate in the glooms of night, They frequent fly in darksome, cloudy days, Oft you may hear aloft in midnight air

Their whistling "scaipe, scaipe" as they onward fare. Not every marsh is haunted by Jack-Snipe. For in sour soil no worms or birds are found, And when sharp frosts still linger in the earth. They come not—but when sot ten'd is the ground By gentle airs and the soft. dropping rain, Their instincts prompt a sure return again. In habits they're eccentric as in flight. At times they early come, then long delay ; Again, their feeding-time is oft at night, Then with the earliest dawn they skim away To center in some quaking, swampy slough, Or brushwood fringing some wet, marshy place. Or to near uplands, where they feed secure, Baffling the gunner in his fruitless chace.

THE PLOVER.

When autumn skies are flash'd with blaze And autumn groves with glory shine, When maples wear their scarlet robes. O'er which the grapevine wreaths entwine. Then far resounds the plovers' cry, As swift o'er upland space they fly.

O'er old Montauk's ravines and slopes, Full oft I've mark'd their legions pass, Now circling, plunging high in air, Now fluttering, hovering o'er the grass. The birds migrating urge their flight In crowded ranks, in serried files, Wheeling, and pausing to alight, Seeking the insect swarms that fill The grasses of the plain and hill.

Those plover tribes, the blackbreast flocks. Ne'er cease their flight o'er pastures wide. Their haunts are by the meadow lands. Where flows and ebbs the salty tide ; And there, in ambush, hid away The fatal fowler seeks his prey.

The golden plover! none more fair Of all the wings that beat the air ;

Birds are they of the bright, warm fields, Darlings of breeze and azure skies, Glad harbingers of early spring, And coming autumn with its dyes. Now swift athwart the grass they flit, How rapid, sweeping on the wing. Now swooping low above the grass, Now brightly glancing as they pass—Arriving when the grass sprouts green, Departing when the airs blow keen.

The upland plover! Sweet its trill, Its operatic, liquid note,

Like the soft breathing of a flute Its symphony in air doth float ;

So low so sweet, one scarce may see This winged minstrel of the air, Till sudden a gray wing floats by, And drops the feather'd lyrist there ; Then o'er the grass lands. far and free Swells out the bubbling harmony!

AUTUMN FLIGHT OF THE BAY SNIPE.

Whither through empty space,

Dost thou, 0 flock, on winnowing wings, Pursue thy migratory journeyings, In tireless, onward race ?

Beneath ye as ye fly,

Float the fleet clouds where brilliant colorings blend. While o'er ye heaven's blue distances extend, The arched, celestial sky.

Far in some Northern home,

Have ye the Spring and Summer seasons known, Beneath the ice floes of Arctic zone,

Where stormy surges foam.

Far out on the sandy shore,

Where the coarse grass waves o'er the reedy swamp, Where the swart Esquimaux hath pitched his camp. Your endless flocks would soar.

But now when Autumn frost

Touches with subtle spirit leaf and flower,

And glows with splendid hues each forest-bower With pomps emboss'd,

Pause here your restless flocks ; Stoop ye from airy flight to earth again,

Cease your migrations o'er the salty main

O'er sands and weedy rocks.

These marshes, far and wide,

Extend their grassy plains and yellow reeds, Sumptuous with fare on which the sea-fowl feeds ;

Then pause, and here abide.

Rich pastures ye invite,

Where sand-flats, mud-banks, fringing the broad bay,

With feasts abundant beckon *ye* to stay,

And on them to alight,

There satiate with rich feast.

When frosty rigors blight the woodland flower, And storms Autumnal o'er the waters lower,

Enshrouding all the East.

Then swift on your pinions rise,
To Summer realms, to tropic regions speed. To warm savannahs and to flowery mead. Beneath fair Southern skies.
There where the palm-groves droop.
And sweet magnolias and the orange grow, Gather your legions by some river's flow, And o'er those meadows sweep.
The Great Creator's hand
Will guide your flight in all your wanderings To fields Elysian, there to fold your wings In the enchanted land.

WILD FOWL SHOOTING.

The fowler ever finds some new delight Amid the varied scenes that Nature spreads; Far from the tumults and the clash of life,
Thro' all her loveliest haunts rejoiced he treads. By lone brooksides. o'er canopied with trees,
He views the gay-hued woodduck wing its flight. By the sand borders of pellucid lakes
He sees the teal and b]ackduck flocks alight ; Bright skies smile o'er reflected in the wave, Soft, winnowing breezes ruffle their expanse, The woods autumnal cast a grateful shade.
The mallard pinions o'er them shift and glance: And here he drops his gay decoys to lure

The hovering flocks, and make destruction sure.
Oft where the breezy bay outspreads its sheet He lurks in ambush 'mid the russet reeds. Casts o'er the blue expanse his searching gaze, To mark the shallows where the blue-bill feeds : Behind him rustle the o'er leaning woods, Above him stretch the over-arching skies, The welcome breezes thrill his sense with joy. The rippled wastes of waters glad his eyes, The restless fowl innumerous sweep around, And the long day with royal spoil is crown'd.
On stormy wings the wild geese squadrons come,

Circling the shallow bays and marshy isles. They hover overhead in phalanx dense, They speed in wedge-like shape, and serried files: In migratory flight these pilgrims pass.

With course unerring thro' the fields of air, Honking and clamoring ere they shyly drop To feast and riot on their dainty fare.

These feather'd wanderers on some Northern coast. Have flown and feasted all the Summer long ; Have cropt the grasses of far Labrador,

Have swept o'er frozen seas in countless throng. There 'mid the barriers of eternal ice,

Where glaciers shine and tidal currents freeze. They framed their nest and rear'd their yellow brood

'Mid desolations bleak of Polar seas ;

And now those restless. migratory flocks

O'er Rocky Mountains pass, o'er ocean coast. Dropping in coves secluded. or wide bays. Still southward pressing, an unnumber'd host. Until at length they fold their wings in rest, Where orange and magnolias shade their nest.

In the far west where grassy prairies stretch Their billows infinite, their vast expanse,

When harvest grain is yellowing o'er the plain. And cornfield banners in the breezes dance; Then come the winged flocks from fields of air, Over the rivers sweep and o'er the lakes,

They feed on wheat fields by the bordering stream ; They swarm o'er lakelet, crystal brook and pool, They greet each dawning with its crimson flush. They come when evening drops its shadows cool, And there the fowler finds supreme delight In daybreak swarmings and in evening flight.

FOWL SHOOTING ON THE ATLANTIC COAST.

Fair scenes I view along the shores serene, The Autumn pomp, the Summer's vivid green, tread the woods embowering the shore.

And view in fancy's dream the scenes of yore : Once more I see migrating geese in air, As forth in serried phalanxes they fare, I see them swooping o'er some outer ledge, Or hovering o'er the salty, yellow sedge ; 1 catch the dusky legions of the brant Sweeping and darting o'er some watery haunt ; Again I view in fancy's magic glass

The blackduck squadrons as they onward pass: I hear the quacking o'er the ample bay Of sprigtail and the widgeon far away, I see the blue-winged teal in whirling flocks Skim o'er the shallows or the inlet rocks ; And wide along the sedgy meadows plain I see the baybirds fluttering again ; There jack curlew and sicklo-bill curlew

Still urge their flight, as in past years they flew The plover, dowitch and the yellowshank Flit o'er each reedy pool or muddy bank, And as they beat with pinions the salt air, I hear their shrilly whistlings everywhere ; So, there for seaons of supreme delight 1 hid in bushy ambush for their flight ; Oft by New England's rock-engirdled verge

I watched the wild fowl speeding o'er the surge. Have marked from day dawn to the close of days. Their wilt procession o'er Long Island bays ; With set decoys, and ambushed in the reed At Barnegat, have viewed their pinions speed ; In Currituck and shores of Chesepeake Have watched their flightin thoroughfare and creek: Full oft by' rock and reef have urged pursuit Of the long columns of the dusky coot; Oft in my little boat, with keen delight, Have raised the gun to check them in their flight.

HAUNTS OF WILD GAME.

FALL DUCK SHOOTING.

The year is waning. and November late,
Paints with its frosty brush the forests green ; Now prairie ponds and shallow sloughs are skimm'd With the thin ice that gleams with silvery sheen The wildfowl now those icy haunts forsake, To seek the running stream, the rivers deep, Where they may gather and enjoy their feast. And o'er the waters sweep.

By the steep banks, where swift the currents run. Or where the open water spreads a lake, They congregate in numbers infinite,
And with their dipping wings the surface break. Fast by the reedy shore securely hid,
The fowlers in their boat thro' bushes peer ; They watch those circling squadrons high in air Wheeling and poising in their fleet career. Now to the channel tide at length they stoop, They hover o'er them with their wings outspread, They skim the waves, uncertain to alight.

As if some menaced danger they would dread. At last the redhead fowl fly fearless down.
No doubtful flight—straight prone their squad-
rons bear ;
Then come the pintails dropping from the clouds. And last the shyer mallard poise in air.
As if in doubt to end their skyward flight.
Long circling, hovering. ere they would alight. Now see the bluebills dart down with a swish,
And now a flock of greenwing'd teal sweep by. Heedless of duckcall, or the fowler's lure,
For they to distant ricefields rapid fly,
Or haply they their swift migrations urge,
To Summer climes beyond the Southern surge. Now as the frosty season rules the year,
And icy floes adown the rivers pass.
When fades all foliage on the forest trees.
And frozen streams shine like the crystal glass ; Then all the flocks on clattering pinions rise.
Passing from slough to pond, from stream to
lake,

Seeking in vain for ancient feeding-grounds, The floating seeds, the acorns to partake, Where they might swim the waves, or pinions
preen,
Skimming the air in regions all serene ; Alas, in vain, the rigid ice hath clos'd,
O'er the swift ripples and the lucent deeps, For bounteous banquet to them is denied.
So the great flock quick in migration sweeps.

THE SCAUP DUCK (BLUEBILL OR BROAD-
BILL), *Fulis'ula Marila.*
Far over ocean surf or breezy bay,
Where the salt tides tumultuous toss the foam ; Far over Western streams that wash the inland realms,
Your restless legions have perennial home. Far o'er Atlantic borders we have mark'd, Your rapid journeyings by each rocky shore, Where rough New England's reefs jut out at sea, And where the Shinnecock spreads sandy floor ; Where Currituck extends its broad expanse, And Chesapeake, Virginia's borders laves, Your myriad, hovering cohorts we have seen Cleaving the air or skimming o'er the waves.
In Western realm, an open-water tribe,
They love to skirt the far mid-river tide ; Safe from the fowler's aim they idly rest,
Or, fitful circling, o'er the waters glide.
Hardy and tough, they like inclement skies.
When the wild billows turbulently roll,
Their pastime then to ride the crested waves,
Diving o'er frothy deeps or sandy shoal.
On bright, still days, when calm the waters sleep. In slothful rest they idly float th' expanse, Or, swiftly swept by currents of the stream, Content they drift where swift the billows dance.
When the broad stream is clogg'd with crystal ice, Sluggish they drift a-near the river-bank,

Floating with tide o'er sunken reef and bar, Till warn'd by hum of life, or engine's clank. They rise in fright and speed afar their flight. Then quick returning, once again alight. The floating ice in shapeless, crystal cakes Crashes and crumbles, piles from shore to shore. Then is the bluebill's carnival of sport ; They climb those ice-floes, floating o'er and o'er. They clambering scale each drifting cake at will. In slothful indolence enjoying rest ; And there in scull boat the hid fowlers drift, And with red slaughter the great flocks molest.

INLAND DUCKS. Far over inland stream and lake The wild-fowl their migration make; First comes that feathered emigrant The mallard duck, a noble game, Rich captive of the fowler's aim. He seeks not the deep-water lake, For there no food he may partake. But finds his home in shallow ooze
'Mid cane-brakes and the muddy sloughs ;
And there with blue-wing teal they pass The spring-time, banqueting on grass.
Thence to their Northern breeding-ground at night. The flocks migrating urge their flight. But when October days are here, And autumn chills the atmosphere, And gathered in is harvest grain, And buckwheat ripens o'er the plain ; When close-cut stubbles of cornfield Their bounteous, golden repasts yield. Then mallard, pintail, broadbill, teal, Across the rich rice-marshes wheel ; But all the wild, deep-water breed Scarce leave profound abyss to feed, For canvas-back and red-heads make Their chosen haunts in deepest lake, And diving in their keen pursuit. Feast on wild celery's juicy root.

THE WOODDUCK. OR SUMMER DUCK.

Most lovely of all birds of air,

That cleave the cloud. or skim the watery space, The wood-duck with its plumage rare, Holds the supremest place.

Thick with rich plumes more gorgeous than the hues

The bird-of-paradise displays,

Gay as the rainbow's glowing arch, Resplendent with its rays.

Brighter than tints imperial spread At sunset, o'er celestial domes, Than tropic birds of sunniest realms. Their flowery fruitful homes,

In vain may bard or Art essay.

Your rare perfections to portray.

A home bird—ne'er to Arctic snows, To Northern reef or Boreal bar, Do their migrating courses tend. Sweeping o'er land and ocean far ; But East and West, where'er a stream Winds o'er the prairies' vast extent, Where'er a brooklet's crystal tide

Pours 'neath the woodland's leafy tent. Where'er a brimming river sweeps.

Or lake, green-hemmed by forest shore. The wood-ducks hover o'er the deeps.

Their flocks the bushy glades explore ; There build the nest. there rear the young.

Their cradles on high branches swung.

So. there where bordering meadows slope

And in the stream their grasses lave. Where trees reflected line the stream,

And lily blossoms gem the wave,

The wood-ducks with their yellow brood.

Luxuriate in the gelid flood.

The willowy, shallow creeks they haunt. Where close the thickets hem the tide, Or by the shores of ample lake,

They revel in the waters wide.

Thro' all the blossoming days of spring. In summer heats, in autumn days, The shadows of their pinions fall
O'er the secluded coves and bays. And when the frosty months draw near They vanish to more genial sphere.

THE SPRIGTAIL DUCK (PINTAIL), *Anas Acuta.*
Swift-flying pilgrims of the realms of air! Few of duck tribe may rival ye in speed ; Perch'd on some grassy tussock of the stream. Ye seem the champions, all bird-flights to lead. With admiration deep we watch ye swim
By muskrat-house. or drift-wood's tangled pile. Calling so softly. with melodious note.
To your mates hovering in the air the while. Greedy for larva. buds, and floating seed. Your luscious banquet, your luxurious feed.
When the snow melts and little rivulets run Thro' the low prairies, forming lake-like sheet. These wary birds on sounding pinions come O'er watery plains to find a safe retreat. The fowlers seek to reach them, all in vain They catch his form and instant upward spring : Circling they soar beyond the weapon's range, And o er broad marsh and timber safely swing.
In his bush stand, concealed in grassy spot, The fowler views the skyward flight in vain. Whistling and chattering speed the feather'd crew. Slow to pitch down to water or to plain. They hover o'er him, whistling as they fly. Gaze down repeating a derisive cry.
Yet there be times when this shy, wary iowl, Seeing the set decoys, will venture round ;
They catch the luring snares, then drop the wing. Eager to settle where such feasts abound. Be all alert ; ye know not whence they come, From sailing cloud or woodland's bowery height :

Sudden a flock may sweep beyond decoys, Whirling in space, and fearful to alight. Then with elusive jump they upward spring. Beating the air with swift-escaping wing.

Far up the frigid coasts of Labrador

Sprigtail and widgeon are but seldom known Only the oceanic fowl frequent

The gelid waters of that Northern zone.

An inland bird, it haunts the Western realm, Skimming o'er ample pond and slough and lake Low o'er the submerg'd timber-lands to sweep. Where the tall beech-woods from their branches

shake

Their nutty banquets. and the oak trees cast The russet acorns, cluster'd in their tops,

And there the clamoring sprigtail, gazing down. Eager for feasts his winnowing pinion drops.

THE CANVASBACK 'DUCK.

When autumn's flushed, celestial skies Pour from full urn their varied hues, And mingled colors of rainbows

The foliage of the groves transfuse ; And every landscape is ablaze

With crimson stain and pomp of gold—A panorama infinite

O'er plain and woodland is unroll'd, Then sportsmen have their carnival

O'er stubble-field and meadow space. Where in the woods the partridge flocks

Have lonely haunt and feeding-place. And where the grouse flocks of the plain

Sweep o'er the harvests of the grain.

Then how delirious is the sport

O'er salty tide and breezy bay,

Where winds continual from the north

Bring the duck-flocks in long array. Then wild geese in a lengthened file

Skim the blue wave or cleave the sky ;

The blackduck. widgeon and the brant Far o'er the water spaces fly.
And noblest game, the canvasback, O'er Chesapeake's broad billows feed.
Hovering or stooping to the feast Where spreads the valisneria seed.
Their legions in the autumn haunt
Potomac and the Chesapeake,
But when the skies inclement frown, Their flocks a milder region seek.
And there, where watery pastures spread. And gentler breezes fan the wave,
They revel in the bounteous fare, And in the temperate billows lave ; But
when the wintry months have pass'd Their tireless migrations press
To Northern wilds and frostier realms, Far up Alaska wilderness,
In California, Oregon,
Their countless multitudes abound In Illinois—by fen and lake
And Iowa their flocks are found. Wherever their choice bulbous fare
Enriches shoal or deepest tide, There, luxurious, they abide,
There beat with winnowing wings the air.

TEAL SHOOTING.
The gay-hued green-wing and the blue-wing teal ! Brilliant in plumage each in
gold and green : No lovelier denizen of earth or air
'Mid the fair feather tribes is seen.
Swift   in their flight, they baffle with their speed The smoking weapon and the
fatal   lead. Swifter than Indian shaft they cleave the air—Swift as electric flash
their flight is sped.
When bright September. with its sunny breath,
Ripens the fruitage and the golden grain-

Enamels all the woodsides with gay flowers, Entwines its rose wreaths over mount and plain. Then first 'neath roseate Summer clouds are seen The hovering, swooping legions of the teal, Skimming o'er tufted wood and lake serene, Heedless of fowier's skiff or shotgun peal.

Far have they journeyed from their Northern home, Where they have rioted and raised the brood ; Winnowed o'er weedy reef and sandy bar, Seeking luxurious and abundant food.

But when the North wind blows with chillier breath. And icebergs crash and floes chafe at the shore. Then these bright-plumag'd children of the air Vanish, some milder regions to explore.

In Middle States and thro' New England realm. Over vast prairies of the fertile West,

By winding river and secluded lake,

The teal-flock gathers. a thrice-welcome guest. Where winds the sparkling brook thro' meadows green,

Or where 'mid bowery groves it joyous sweeps. Where rolls the river past its bushy fringe, The teal its holiday, rejoicing, keeps.

There, o'er some muddy bank or reedy isle, By sheltered shore or green. secluded cove, They bask in sunshine, drowsily at rest,

Or on the wing flit swiftly thro' the grove, Or to some haunt of wild rice or of oat
On rapid-beating winnowing pinions float.
How oft in happy, long-departed years,

Have I, at Stooling point or Northwest edge At thy green shores, 0 Bay of Barnegat !

Watch'd for teal flocks. swift-darting o'er the sedge,

When the first roseate blushes of the day

Flush'd all the East, engilding cloud and land,

Ere blackduck and the widgecn winged their flight,

The early teal would hover o'er my stand. *My* set decoys would lure their searching *eye*—They whirl, they circle, and in mid-air die !

WILD-GEESE.

Sailing in the solemn midnight underneath the frosty moon,
I can hear the clanging pinions of each shadowy platoon,
Hear the winged hosts commotion, marching to the Northern Ocean,
File on file, rank on rank, speeding to some reedy bank,
Oozy fens or marshes gray, far up Baffin's icy bay; Honking, clamoring in their flight
under the black clouds of night.
Sailing thro' the noonday heavens, their battalions 1 discern,
Wedge-like or in open column, still toward the North they turn ;
Straight o'er Jersey's sandy borders, o'er Long Island's sea-like sound.
Past Montauk or bleak Fire Island, north, still north unerring bound ;
High above the loftiest pine tree, far above the stateliest oak,
Still unflagging their dark pinions beat the air with steady stroke.
Winging over wastes of ocean, over voyaging ships they pass,
Where from reeling mast the shipboy notes them with the uprais'd glass,
And the fisher in his dory drops his line to view their flight,
And the baffled fowler gazes, hopeless, till they fade from sight
Inland over plain and pasture, over mountain. wood and stream,
Onward speeds the long procession, northward the swift pinions gleam.
Through the rough, dark months of winter, in what sunny clime,
     'Mid green lagoons and savannahs, pass'd ye the delicious
     time ?

Haply amid verdurous islands where the Mexic billows smile,
'Mid sweet flower-glades and gay plumage ye would riot all the while;
Haply amid red flamingoes, hovering o'er some lilied lake,
Where the aloe droops its branches and the palms their branches shake.

MIGRATIONS OF THE WILD-GEESE.
Under the midnight moon
I hear the clanging pinions of the geese, Quick-flapping, that never seem to cease.
Swifter than duck or loon.
These wing'd hosts have come From Southern lagoon and from limpid lake,
From ocean borders where the billows break,
Their sunny Winter home.
I see them high in air.
Touch'd by the glancing moonbeams in their flight. Skimming athwart the floating clouds of night,
As on they ceaseless fare.
Sweet, genial scenes they knew Where gay magnolias wav'd their snowy bells, And orange groves were fragrant with their smells.
And green palmettos grew.
By each enchanting haunt,
Where birds of gorgeous plumage fill'd the wood. Where red flamingoes in the shallows stood.
And flew the duck and brant.
There, in that temperate zone,
The geese-flocks o'er the grassy meadows fed Their yellow goslings, o'er the marshes led
In haunts to man unknown.
And when the airs of Spring Will breezy o'er the wide savannahs pass, Wide over wood, and lakes as clear as glass.
The wild-geese ply the wing.

O'er Currituck they speed,
O'er Chesapeake's blue watery plain they sweep, O'er Barnegat their journey still they keep,
Or pause where they feed.
Right onward, onward still,
They skirt the level sandy-bordered coast:
Fast o'er Long Island bays, that feathered host.
O'er beach and sand-dune hill,
Hastes the unwearied flight.
O'er Maine's bold shores they winnowing sweep.
Neer deigning to alight.
Until they reach those seas; The icy banks of Baffin's ample bay.
Thro' Belleisle Strait they urge their onward way
Where lakes and rivers freeze.
Far up the Greenland beach, Amid the lonely, marshy solitudes,
The wild-geese rest and rear their callow brood.
Beyond the fowler's reach.

FLIGHT OF WILD GEESE—'87.
High up in upper field of air
I note   your serried phalanx on its way ;
Now   rank on rank your winnowing squadrons press, And now a wedge-like host display. A soft south breeze stirs overhead,
Peconic Bay in slumber sleeps in rest : There is no ripple o'er its blue expanse, No foam-wreath on its breast :
The withered Autumn leaves on Shelter Isle Without a rustle settle to the ground. The curling smokes on many a village roof
Rise not, the calm is so profound.
Better you like a stormy blast,
A wrathful hurricane the earth to shake, To help your flapping pinions on their flight
O'er forest range and lake ;
For slow your laboring cohorts sail

As if wing-weary on your journeyings far, From Belle Isle Strait and dreary Labrador You pass o'er craggy cliff and bar,

Where all the Summer long in reedy swamp Hath been your breeding place and camp. Upward our wondering eyes behold

This pilgrim apparition of the skies,

This grand procession painted 'gainst the clouds. 'Gainst morning cloudlets flash'd with roseate dyes.

1 list your honking. clarion notes,

Like bugles cheering the mad fight's career! How sweet and flute-like, tremulous they fall, Soften'd by distance to the ear.

Vainly, close hid, in lurking boat.

Or in thick ambush of the sedgy shore, The fowler may his deadly weapon raise,

His leaden hail on your wide ranks to pour I Pass on, brave birds, far down the Jersey beach, But linger not in Barnegat's great bay, Nor pause at Currituck or Pimlico,

For cruel gunners there obstruct the way ; But urge thy gleamy wings to Southern clime. To calm lagoons. where orange grove and lime With golden fruits are ever in the prime ; Where pelicans and red flamingo flocks Hover in peace o'er sands and weedy rocks. Oft in the past in such wild fowl retreat

Have I found robust health and pastimes sweet.

THE WILD .SWAN.

Far dost thou come, 0 bird of noblest form, From stormy regions of the Arctic home; From icy floes where walrus herds resort,

And the black seal-flocks tumble in the foam : Where prowls the white bear o'er the icy fields, And rise the snow huts of the Esquimaux ; Swart tribes are they who dare the frothy surf,

Pursuing victims with the spear and bow,

There o'er the drifting, far extending snows The shadows of thy wings sweep o'er the floes. In Western realms thy race is nigh extinct. Realms where thy flocks once fill'd the air of
yore,
Haunting the lakes and rivers in great flocks. The great bayous and unfrequented shore ; But now, alas! thy swarming files forsake Those ancient haunts in river, bog and lake !
In ages past thy beauty charm'd the world.
Great nobles, where their shapely barks were
built,
Would seek perfection in thy perfect shape, Modeled with skill, resplendent with their gilt. In such fair bark went Cleopatra forth
To conquer Antony and rule the earth.
Far off in Southern haunt, in broad lagoon, In sunny isles. grand archipelagos
Where the white sands with crystal shells are strewn.
And each green glade with golden fruitage glows : Where soars the palm-trees and magnolias rise.
And gorgeous flowerets shine like brilliant skies. There 'mid perennial blooms thy home shall be Thy snowy pinions sweep o'er shore and sea.

" Hunting is the noblest exercise,
Makes men laborious, active, wise ;
Brings health, and doth the spirits delight, It helps the hearing and the sight ;
It teacheth arts that cannot slip
The memory, good horsemanship,
Search, sharpness and defense,
And chaseth all ill habits hense."
JOHNS

THE SHARP-TAILED GROUSE.

Long o'er the dreary desert men have toil'd, Where only the wild sage-bush fill'd the sand; At length, in Southern Idaho their camp Is pitched—an oasis of hunter's land; It is the game-land, in a grass'd plateau.

By a clear stream that sparkles down the dale. Fring'd by the quaking aspens and the hedge Of bear-berries, prodigal through the vale ;

And here the whirring sharp-tail grouse have made Their chosen haunts, in thickets of the glade.

In earliest spring-time, ere the grass is green,

Ere tender foliage robes the branches sere, The grouse from woods of cedar and of pine (Where they have passed the winter-time of year) Descend in packs to skim the verdurous plain,

'Till frosts invade to drive them back again. There the maternal bird selects her nest,

Not in dense groves, nor 'mid the grasses green Of upland valleys, but where roses wild

With matted leaves the hidden refuge screen ; And here the warrior-sentinel, her mate,

Watches the nest, with loving pride elate.

Their camp is in a park of green expanse,

Fring'd by a willowy brook—a crystal sheet—Where ravines ope their aspen-border'd gates,

And blacktail deer resort for dim retreat. Far off rise peaks capp'd with eternal snow,

While 'neath the snow-line piny forests grow. Early and bleak along the mountain range

Comes the stern winter, with its tempests black ; Then from the lowland valleys and the streams

Hasten the grouse-packs in assembled pack, To choose their home-haunt for the winter-time, Sheltered by woodlands from the frosty rime.

Here perch'd on pines they seek a friendly roost,

And here the lawless poacher comes to stay : Then all the startled flocks speed off in fright.

But at the dusk return, a helpless prey.

When deep snows sweep the mounts, those hardy birds
Burrow in snow-drifts to escape their foe
Or. when the thickets may not screen from storrit, They 'scape the blizzard, buried in the snow; But when the frost forms all the snows a crust The imprisoned birds dig tunnels that may save. And there, close-packed, in safety they repose, Though oft they perish in that frosty grave.

THE NESTING AND FEEDING ROOSTS OF
THE WILD PIGEON.
The blue, wild pigeons seek the sunless roosts In lonely forests of far Michigan,
In deepest, inmost, unfrequented wilds
Of Minnesota and Kentucky realms,
In Indiana groves. Ohio wastes;
And further South. in Mississippi haunts,
They thickly congregate in earliest Spring To build the cradles for their callow broods, And late in year their feeding roosts to seek.
Years since in utmost East those purple flocks Swift-winnowing in myriad flights the air
Hovered o'er forest-glooms and harvest plains, Where ripe the yellow grain-fields scatter'd seeds. There rioting where corn-fields wav'd their flags, Where oat-
fields shook their ruddy pennoncells, Where crimson
strawberries painted the green turf, Where hedge-side
weeds their seeded tributes cast. Where luscious blue-berries lavish d a repast,
And chief where oaks with acorns strew'd the
earth.
But later still when emigration pass'd
Onward to Western plains and prairie-lands, And axe and plow the virgin acres ope'd,
Then to those new-found fields the pigeon-flocks In endless multitudes sought bounteous homes. In the Spring-time they seek some calm retreat,

Where miles of forest stretch their bowery realms. And here they build the nest and rear the young. Here tender grass and undergrowth die out, And earth is strewn with wither'd branch of trees. Broken by weight of birds that roost above, And then the forest trees decay and die,

As if the girdling axe had sapt their cores ; And here the farmers, greedy for the spoil Encamp'd beneath that nursery immense, Engather up the crush'd and dying birds,

That fall by thousands from the o'erladen boughs 'Twas perilous then to pass beneath those woods. Under these myriad crowding. falling flocks, That snapt the branch by weight of multitudes. Then hawks and buzzards sailing in the air, Seize the young squabs, and riot in rich feast. While like the thunderous roaring of the surf, The tumult of their pinions shakes the air !

But when October kindles the great woods. Flushing the oaks and beech-trees with their blaze, The flocks return and with their crowded roosts People the branches where the beech-nuts grow. And thrill the air with flutterings and sounds; And when the generous nut-harvest fails,

The flocks in numerous processions pass,

Where milder Southern climes give welcome homes.

THE VALLEY QUAIL OF CALIFORNIA.

Far over Californian realm.

Far down the sultry Mexic coast,

The valley quail o'er mount and vale Assembles—a shy, countless host.

Though haunting the sea-level line, It finds a home on upland space,

Happy in torrid. shadeless glare; Happy in cool, secluded place.

Whose arbors of wild rose and grape, The sycamore with festoons drape,

Alike to him the settler's glebe,

Or lofty hill-top far away

Whether he feeds on strawberry feast.

Or dry grass-seed, in sterite clay ; Forever sleek and cheerful where

The scantiest herbage spreads its fare. Forever busy is the quail,

Fore'er on wing save in the night Ne'er sits with ruffled, drooping plumes, But ever is alert in flight :

Its plumage rich, and sweet the note That, various. bubbles from its throat. Its bevies over acres spread,

O'er stubble-field, or sundried grass; Out of the cactus patch they spring,

From sumac clump or rocky pass ; And in each canon dim we hear,

At morn, at eve, the clanging strife Of fluttering wings, and see the air

Fill'd with blue lines of feather'd life. Step cautious gunner—for their spring,

As forth they burst on whirring wing, Will cheat thee—for in white sage brush.

Wreath'd with the garlands of the pea. They hidden lie—and forth will whiz.

With whistling chirpings as they flee ; Or, happy where grow poppies red,

Or wild buckwheat with flowrets spread, They lurk—then quick on buzzing wing

The baffling darlings upward spring! 'Tis a fair scene that charms the *eye*

The earth ablaze with blooms unknown, Skies purer that all foreign skies

Bird songs of unfamiliar tone,

      Views of green slopes that roll serene, Long undulations. blue and
      green. Until they end in far-off hills.

Whose peaks the mind with wonder fills.

THE WILD TURKEY.

These noble birds that did abound Innumerous over Northern ground—Victims so oft to northern sport—Now seek in southern realms resort ; In Mexico, in Texas State,

Their numbers are supremely great. Where strutting. gobbling flocks are seen, Most frequent in the forests green, And there oft thunder-like are heard, The flappings of the turkey bird.

Seek them where gloomy shadows fall Beneath the woodland dim and tall; In the dense alder-brakes. or where The dark pines lift their spears in air. Where slow or winding rivulet creeps. Or swift thro' bushy ravine sweeps. Hid in tall grass that spreads around, Your call deceptive. faintly sound,

And soon you hear each answering note. From the embowering thickets float Soon will perceive the cautious game Step forth—then steady be your aim.

A hunter. ere the dawning day, Flushes with blaze the forest's way, Selects his ambush near a wood, Where roosting. rest the noble brood. 'Tis lovely morn of early spring, That gilds the earth with blossoming ; The violets and daisies white.

Enamel earth with colorings bright, The red-buds with their pinkish spray, Entwine the trees with garlands gay ; The humid air holds odors still,

Of wild-plum blooms o'er plain and hill. While snowy dogwood blossoms cling To branch, the bridal-wreaths of Spring. Then all the wood-bowers teem with life, With   wild-wood melodies, are rife, Then sudden from a dense tree top.

On dashing wing the turkeys drop, Skim in wide circles down the air, Then sink to earth the feast to share, While quick the fowler's shot is heard And bleeding, struggling dies the bird,

WILD TURKEY HUNTING.

It was the morning of a sweet spring day,
When all the woods were rob'd in perfect green. When earliest flowers were faded where they grew. Daisies and violets, children of the Spring; The red-buds rare that garlanded the trees Had cast their roseate blossoms to the earth, Yet still the air their dying fragrance held ; The song-birds filled the air with melodies, Fluting their varied liquid symphonies
Sweet operas of woods, blithe concerts of the wild. A scarlet songster from his oak-tree crown Pour'd o'er the hunter his full anthems rich, When silence deep the woodlands would pervade.

*   *   *   *

Ambushed in leafy covert long he sat,
Watchful and patient—yet no gobbler came; At length the sharp sound of a broken twig Reaches his ear—and he is all alert,
And as three deer stepped forth he raised the gun, But no—'tis season close—he spares the shot ; Slow and unharm'd the three does saunter'd past. Listening and cropping dainty buds of vine, And soon with lazy step they vanished by.
Now sun is up, bespangling forest leaves,
And scattering pearly dewdrops on the grass. Ah ! there he is!—the object of his search—Moveless as statue in the edge of woods;
He struts, he gobbles, but he moves not near. And so the cautious hunter, creeping low,
Seeks closer blind beneath a thicket "s screen, There waits with bated breath and ready gun. And lists the victim's gobble sound again ;

And he replies with three short, smothered yelps. Again the gobble and the answering cries, And still afar the wary creature lurks. At last the hunter moves to open glade. At edge of which a bushy hide is found, And there in perfect ambush prone he lies. Again the gobble and responsive yelp! As nearer, nearer comes the welcome sound; The hunter's nerves are strung in thrills intense. Two minutes pass—it seems to him an age— Then comes a glimpse of white, tall-lifted head Above the tangled bushes of the glade. 'Tis still a moment—then it gliding comes ; And soon with stealthy, striding step moves on, The glossy form of this wild knight of woods Clad in his feather'd panoply of bronze.

Ere he has reach'd the glade he sudden stops ; He stands erect, quick glancing all around. As listening to some warning of a foe, His folded pinions clasp'd like plated mail. The hunter knows his quarry has but come To peep into the glade and then pass on : So there's a rapid glance along his gun— . His silver bead fits truly at the notch, Settling exact upon the victim's breast;

Then quick is trigger touch'd, a thund'rous crash ! A whirl of feathers and outspread of wings, Convulsive struggle. and the gobbler falls; One tremor and one gasp—the victim dies!

FIELD SPORTS IN EARLY DAYS.
TO S. C. CLARKE.
In past years we together rang'd.
Dear cousin, far o'er prairies wide, Plains of illimitable space,
Like billowy sweep of ocean tide.
Immense those *grassy* worlds outspread.
Dotted with groves by creek and lake. Groves like fair islands of the seas,
Isles that the rolling surface break. To the horizon's hazy line
They stretch, with tall grass waving green. Enamell'd with their snow-white flowers,
Like surf o'er ocean's face serene,
Then all that spacious realm was thrill'd
With bird life in each shady wood, Birds trilling flute-like melodies,
Enchanting the dim solitude.
Endless the game in those old days
To tempt the hunter's zealous guest ; The partridge drum'd in densest grove.
Or hover'd o'er its hidden nest ;
The grouse flocks swept the prairies far. They sprang from tussocks of the grass.
Their pinions beat the empty air,
And swift o'er harvest stubble pass'd
The wild ducks haunted swamp and creek,
They gather'd o'er each muddy slough, Their rapid pinions swept the plain.
Their legions o'er the marshes flew.
The canvasback, the mallard tribe,
The woodduck, spoon-bill and the teal. The blackduck and the widgeon flocks,
O'er every reedy pool would wheel.
The red deer, startled from his haunt,
Through thicket dense and grove would speed, Tossing his antlers in the chase,
Defying hunter and his steed.
Those were the years for sportsmen's zeal.

For rich reward and sumptuous spoil ; Not far to seek for noble game.
Not unrewarded vvas the toil.
But Time, they tell, hath wrought a change. The pigeon flocks now scarce are seen. Extinct are all the bison herds, And vanish'd have the hunted deer. The great grouse flocks are thin and few, Those million ducks seek "pastures new,- Yet hunters keen find pastime still, With patient toil, consummate skill.

DEER.
Far in the hemlock forests of Maine
And where thick the pine woods weave a shade. The noble stag with branching horn Flits thro' the densest wood arcade ; By Moosehead Lake far up the waste, And where Penobscot's sources rise, The forest hunter takes his stand, And in the tangled thicket lies; There waits in ambush for the deer, That comes to taste the brooklet wave. Unconscious of the lurking foe. So eager in the fount to lave
Then quick the rifle's deadly aim Slaughters the unwary forest game. Where thick the Adirondack groves, Outstretch a wilderness of woods, Casting a sombre endless shade O'er placid lake and river-floods,
The hunter comes with gun and hound To seek his prey in that lonely ground: He knows by tracks in the grassy land, By broken twig or hoof-print there
That dappled hind comes there for rest And crops the feed in that chosen lair: No sign may escape the hunter's eye. So the wary deer comes there to die !

Where the Southern plantations spread The wild deer thro' dense forests rove ; They speed thro' thicket and tangled glade, Cropping the grass in shaded grove, And there the eager cavalier

With whoop and hulloo follows the chase Cheering the fierce pursuing hound In headlong dash, and tireless race.

In long past years, ere emigrants pour'd In countless bands o'er the distant West, Beyond the Rocky Mountain slopes

And o'er the prairie realms they pressed, The early settlers and trappers found In trackless wastes abundant game, The stately elk, the grizzly bear,

The antelope, the mountain sheep,

That scoured each plain and woodland-lair ; And there the stag with antlers crown'd, There in each ravine and prairie-plain, Roamed free in all that forest ground And there were by the ardent hunter slain.

HAUNTS OF THE DEER.

Far up 'mid Adirondack fastnesses,

Where Nature spreads her grand, sublimest scenes, White torrents foaming down the rugged slopes, Wild gulch, dark chasms and the steep ravine, Thick, towering forests of the evergreen, The hunter loves to track the noble deer, And follow with his hounds that flying game, Here builds his bowery camp ; his fragrant couch The tender tips of some tall hemlock tree ; His drink the crystal waters of the brook, His food the venison haunch or fowls of air, And here far-off from vex'd turmoils of life, Far from its traffic and its greed of gold, Content and happy pass his healthful years.

Grand here the scenes that burst upon his view, Gray, splintered cliffs and pinnacles sublime,

Shaggy with sombre woods and solemn shades In whose recesses lurk the bear and wolf ; Fair too the scene outspreading far and near, Broad valleys verdurous with meadows green, The winding rivers with their silvery sheen,

The tumbling brook that leaps from crag to crag. The wide, undimpled lake. whose lucent sheet Reflects the bending forests of the shore ; While high above him spreads a canopy, Of heavenly azure and celestial light ;

Where wandering breezes fill the dusky groves With hymnings tuneful as angelic choirs Or chant of organs in Cathedral domes. No wonder then his soul finds deep delight 'Mid scenes so fair, *in* wonder-land so grand, When every waking hour is full of joy,

Seeking the browsing deer from wood to wood ! Ere dawn hath dappled with its roseate hues

The dome of skies, or touch'd with flame the clouds, The hunter with his hounds forsakes the camp, And thro' the darken'd forest takes his way. He tramps thro' briary swamp and alder brake. Glides thro' the vaulted arches of great woods, O'er upland slopes and granite crag and cliff, Then lies at ambush in some run-way haunt, While far away his noble stag-hounds range.

HUNTING THE DEER (Cervus *Virginianus.)*

These graceful creatures in the long-past years Swarmed o'er all regions of the continent, And still exist where forests have been spared, And wanton rapine have not thinned their flocks. In sections of New York they yet abound,

In Adirondack wildernesses wild.

But chiefly haunt the forest depths of Maine, Finding retreats in evergreen arcades,

By shore of lake and at the river's edge

Where they elude the hunter's fateful quest. Hiding in pathless woods and tangled swale ;

But even there they meet remorseless foes, Where loggers grim and ruthless lumbermen Hew with their axes the entangled woods. Unsparing, slaughtering all the woodland game ; For these rude spoilers, in their lawless moods, Slay wandering caribou and browsing deer, In every season close of the protected year. They watch each runway by the lakelet marge. In leafy ambush lurking for the game. The prey that comes the limpid waves to taste. Or plunging, riot in the cooling tides ; But chief these cruel slaughterers collect, Where billowy hillocks of the drifting snows Fill every icy hollow of the waste,

And then when crusts and drifts obstruct the way. These rough marauders on their snowshoes borne, Entice the deer and slaughter them at will.

The honest hunter in some forest grove. At brink of lake or by a river shore,

Lies ambushed while he listens for the yelp

Of the fleet deer-hounds as they range the waste. Then when the pack give warning with their cries He knows the quarry are aroused in flight. And hid by rock or tree he takes his stand. Ready with rifle and with deadly aim ; But if the deer in lakelet seeks escape He follows, paddling swift his light canoe. O'ertakes the victim swimming for its life.

And those bright lakes, deep woods and breezy hills, No spot in nature is so passing fair. Whether the groves their Summer tresses wear, Or draped with colors of Autumnal hues ; So there is work for hunter's deftest skill, For true foot, strong arm and the keenest eye. For him who best can rouse the lurking deer. Bringing him to bay, raise high victorious cheer. And bear the spoil triumphantly to camp.

CARIBOU HUNTING IN A CANADIAN WINTER.

On with the snow shoes, for the drifts lie deep, Gather'd in hollows, crested on steep ; For in glooms of untrodden forest land,

Where rise the fir branches and hemlocks grand. These great stags of the North have chosen haunt. Where never a glimmering sunbeam may slant.

Awake, 0 sleepers, while stars are yet bright,

Ere the first gleams of day shine out on the night. Then all rally forth from the hunter's camp O'er the glass-like surface driftings to tramp.

Onward, right onward presses the band, Till the caribou's yard is close at hand In wild forest glade. where many a hoof Has trampled a space 'neath the forest roof ; And there assembled, they feed at will, In safe retreat from the rifle's skill ;

Vain trust, for the hunters the haunt have found, And in fatal ambush the yard surround! Grand scene to witness I surpassing strange, Gigantic bulls at point-blank range, Flapping their huge ears with the cold, Like slothful cattle in farmer's fold, While the cows are browsing the fir tops sweet. Trampling the grass with cloven feet. Secure from harm in this woodland retreat.

At given signal the rifles flash,

> The bullets in bone and sinew crash, And all is tumult, terror and blood,

While the virgin snows blush crimson with blood. Some of these forests cattle in death lie low, Some wounded in drifts flounder to and fro, Bellowing savagely, menacing fight If antler'd males, in furious might. While those who escape the deadly lead Far off in trackless thickets have fled. The sharp knife bleeds, the prostrate slain. The rifle, the tomahawk end their pain,

But beware, 0 hunter! draw not too near With empty rifle the caribou deer,
For the wounded quarry, mad for strife, May charge the hunter at peril of life !

MOOSE, (A *ices Americanus).*
This noble creature in departed years
Rang'd free the Northern regions of the land, Ere came white hunters with the hound and gun. Their browsings to molest in depth of woods: The deadly rifle, the breech-loading steel Then woke no echoes in primeval groves, The trapper was unknown in solitudes,
And only the red Indian sought the herds, And with the spear and arrow slew the game : Far as the Northern land has been explored, Far as the Arctic regions stretched immense. Their clattering hoofs the forest soil impress'd.
The Great Lakes limited their southward range, And in these later days but few remain :
Some remnants still by Fundy's lonely bay. In furthest precincts of Maine's wilderness,
And round the Hudson Bay, yet range the wilds. The forests dense and willow-tangled swamps. In those far regions were their native haunts, Where their great length of limb might serve them
well

> To reach the twigs of maple or of birch,
> Or crop aquatic plants by sedgy shore.

In Summer-time the moose frequents the swamp. Or low grounds near the marge of brook or lake, Loving to wade far out the ice-cold wave,
Feeding on broad-leav'd plants that float the stream, And there the lurking Indian finds his prey. But when the Winter snows o'erspread the earth, The moose-gangs seek the shelter of the woods. Cropping the clinging mosses of the trees, Browsing the tender saplings and the buds.

In the bleak North, where March winds sweep the waste,
And the deep snows are crusted o'er with ice, Hunters. with knapsack and the rifle-gun,
The thick woods penetrate and build their camp. They seek the moose-yard trodden in the drifts, And in each early morn, ere yet the sun
Had softened the thin crusts that glaze the snow, They send their hounds across the crystal track. And borne on snowshoes follow hard behind. When the fierce dogs assail on every side, The frightened moose-herds, dashing in escape, But quick their hoofs break thro' the brittle plain, And helpless stand the animals at bay, While all the yelping packs the herd surround, And the unsparing balls the struggles end.

HUNTING THE MOOSE.

To hunt the moose-herd calls for rare display, Of highest qualities of Indian life ;
Endurance, caution, keenness of the sight, Knowledge of woodcraft in the forest chase. Are all more needful to secure the game, Than daring heart, or deadly rifle aim.
Far in the West, the Indians, in "moose-drive," Wage cruel slaughter with the death-doom'd prey : And ere each raid a grand moose-dance is held, With feasts to celebrate the wild foray.

Then when October colors all the woods,

The savage camps march forth with all their train.
For then moose herds have left their woodland haunts
To seek their mates across the grassy plain.
Then in some chosen place, where moose abound, Men form a cordon-ring of ample space,
And with loud cries and beat of hollow drum, They drive the herds to some surrounded place ; Fierce, with sharp spear and feather'd shaft they
slay,

The captive herds and various forest game ; And if some grizzly bear becomes their spoil They rend the air with triumphant acclaim. At other times men hide in mountain pass,

Or path that leads to where cool rivulets meet, While others to this gorge or pass of death

Drive the doom'd herds whence there is no retreat. At times, when all the male moose champions

come.

In desperate, duel conflicts they engage. So fierce are they in wooings and in fight. So fill'd with furious ire and jealous rage,

That scarce they pause to browse upon the fare. And fail in strength—so he that stalk'd, a king, Thro' the September forest, proud of mien. Now in November's but a craven thing A weakly. half-starv'd, enervated wretch, That now would scarcely combat with a cur. But sulks and mopes in some secluded lair.

Moose in Atlantic States and Canada.

Are fast forsaking their choice haunts of old, But now seek refuge past the Rocky Mounts, Idaho, and Alaska's regions cold.

The Indians tell that in some Western wilds,

From ancient homes have vanish'd the great game,

They fled to forest recesses afar,

Since   to all haunts destroying white men came. The red men oft with pitfall and with   trap, Capture the herds, but chief they lie in wait, Hid in some bushy ambush by a stream,

And there the thirsty moose herds meet their fate.

LOGGERS AND HUNTERS.

In the grand forest-realms of Maine, Aroostock wilds and Moosehead Lake, Amid the gloomy pines they dwell, Their rustic logging camps they make. Far thro' Canadian wilderness With axe and saw invade the waste, Thro' cedar swamps and hemlock press, The towering woods to devastate ; And Adirondack groves of oak Ring with their shots, and axes' stroke.

By lakelet lone, and bush-girt pond, They pitch the camp in Autumn time, Now felling the majestic fir,

And now the trunks of spruce sublime; But ever have they pastimes rare, By river bank and rushing stream, Casting the line for springing trout, Or where the leaping salmon gleam.

But more intense the woodmen's joy, To wait and watch where Caribou Wallow and wade in forest bath; Where lotus and white lilies grew ; For there the rifle's deadly aim Would immolate the forest game.

But when the Winter snows lie deep And frosty drifts the plains outspread, And crackles the encrusted ice

Beneath the moose-hoof's crushing tread; When all the yarded herds collect,

• Tramping high hillocks of the snows, Feeding on bark and juicy buds, Unconscious of surrounding foes,

Then hunters, on their snow-shoes light. Forsaking sleds and logging team. Assemble   at that place of doom. And with the volleying death-shots slay The helpless victims brought to bay. Then redden'd are the snows with gore,

The slaughter'd herd fall thick around, In vain the mad rush to escape,
In vain the frantic leap and bound!

THE CANADIAN VOYAGEUR AND HUNTER.

In the old Canadian forests,
Woods primeval, dim and grand, From the realm of lake and river, The backwoodsman's chosen land Comes the stalwart voyageur, Chanting songs of ancient France, Songs, his warlike ancestors
Sang when wielding sword and lance. In that far Canadian country,
By the river's glassy wave,
Stands the hamlet of his people,
Home and field, the church and grave. Singing, dancing merrily ;
But the music and the dances, Could not woo the voyageur,
Lure him from his hunting pastimes. From his peltries and his fur ;
O'er the swift, tumultuous river. Lakes far-stretching, lakes sublime.
Have his glancing paddles answer'd To the merry boatsman's chime, He hath cross'd the Indian country
Floated down Missouri's tide. Where Nebraska pours its billow,
Where the swift Platte currents glide; With the Osage and the Pawnee,
Winnebago and Sioux,

    He hath floated, he hath hunted,
    Rioting with savage crew.

With their life of savage freedom.
With their careless merriment, He hath ever been enchanted,
Living in their wigwam tent. He hath chosen for the bridal

HAUNTS OF WILD GAME.

Some brown daughter of the chief, Maiden charming with her blushes, Warlike with her arrow-sheaf.
Clad in garment of the buckskin,
Fring'd and ornamented o'er, Girdled with a sash of crimson, That his knife and hatchet bore. With his rifle at his shoulder,
He would forth to wood and plain, And the crashing of his weapon, Would proclaim a victim slain.
O'er the burn'd and blacken'd prairies, Where the Indian fires had been, In the foot-tracks of the bison
He would follow fast and keen ;
Follow the great brown moose-herds
Clattering fast with cloven hoof ; And the grizzly bear affrighted
From his chase would keep aloof. By the forks of some great river,
He would build his lodge afar, Ready for the hunt or revel,
For the feast or for the war. Happy in that Indian country,
Loving all the savage ways,
He would pass his prime of manhood,
To the ending of his days.

THE FAR WEST.

Westward, in fancy's mystic dream, we pass, Where Mississippi rolls its mighty tide, " Father of Waters." swift, majestic, grand, Pressing its onward march to   meet the sea, Thro' the great valley, garden of the world. From Alleghany peaks that hem the East. To distant Rocky Mountains of the West, Thousands of tributary streams converge To swell, 0 parent river, thy broad tide; Such other valley, with its affluent soil Exists not on this vast, terrestrial globe!

154

On o'er the plains, the illimitable plains !

TrapperA and hunters old, whose rugged lives Have pass'd, amid those boundless, prairie realms, Amid wild buffaloes and Indian tribes,

Pronounce that name with reverential awe ;

It calls to mind remembrance of rough scenes, Of famines. feastings, battles and escapes ; So travelers now look o'er those seas of grass As if to note those savage, whooping bands

With feather'd plume, and rattling spear and shield, Sweep o'er the wastes and raise their war-whoop

wild,

While howl'd the wolf, and sped the antler'd deer And elk and antelope the pastures rang'd.

The plains are passed—the parch'd and sunscorch'd plains!

And now we gaze on Rocky Mountain scenes ; Here 'mid the solitude of Nature's sleep,

Rough, rocky peaks rise to a dizzy height, Their bases with a sombre foliage clad,

Which upward dwindles into thorny shrubs, Ending in naked rock and snow-capped peak ; How wild and desolate its Winter scene !

Then pendent crystals hang from frowning ledge. The gloomy forest bends 'neath mantle white, While high up 'mid the crags (where shines the sun Cheerless and cold o'er all the frozen world). The howling storm is laden with the snows That sweep like fleecy mist the summits bleak, To sink in drifts behind those granite walls.

Grand here the view from some high-soaring cliff, O'er the vast plain extended far away!

Rivers and streams thro' rolling prairies wind. Sparkling in light, like silvery ribbons spread ; Fring'd with dark timber-belts and terrac'd rows Of bluffs, that upward reach to elevated plains, Plains that roll off like ocean billows, sown With flowery blooms, unshaded by a tree.

MORNING, NOON AND NIGHT.

Far up the Mississippi's Northern land.

'Mid the primeval forests grand and wild,

Itaska lake in placid beauty smiles

With mighty soaring cliffs around it piled: It is the crystal source whose currents glide To swell the Mississippi's downward tide.

The waters here are crystaline in flow

Studded with verdant islands, in whose shades 'Tis sweet to ramble in the dim arcades,

Shady at eve and bright in midday glow.

There o'er the limpid waves the wild fowls sweep, The snow-white swan, the mallard and the teal, Where the grim wolf and deer flit o'er the plain, Or from their leafy coverts cautious steal.

At morn the hunter view'd the stag and elk, Cropping the grass while dewdrops wet their sides. With graceful smoke curl'd from the Indian camps Or Indians launched canoes across the tides : It was a lovely morn that lit the scene.

Shining o'er waters and the forests green.

A noontide panorama fair to view!

No breath of breezes stirring o'er the space The grass o'er level prairies motionless,

The song birds chanting in each sylvan place.

The deer had paused to taste the running stream.

On a dead branch a great bald eagle stood, Then spread his pinions soaring up the skies. His keen eyes glancing over stream and wood. Gay butterflies and wild bees flew o'er flowers, And peace and silence reigned in earth and air, As if boon nature offered up a prayer ;

While far away the Mississippi's surge,

Faded away beyound the horizon's verge. Sudden, anon, the landscape faded fast, As the sun set, bright clouds streamed o'er the skies,

Decked in their gorgeous pencilings of light ; And bright the evening star did then arise The setting sun in twilight bathed the founts,

His last beams shining over vales and mounts. The moon ascended to her regal throne.

And thro' the groves was heard no wildbird tone The doe and fawn to grassy couch had gone, The bird, the breeze, the wave had ceased a trill, A mantle of sweet silence hush'd each hill, As midnight spread its shadow o'er the earth ; The moon sank down, the stars illum'd the sky, Each voice was in the Indian's wigwam hush'd. Warriors asleep dream'd of their victories. At times a wailing breeze thro' forest gush'd, An owl was hooting in the hollow tree,

The only sounds. the splash of leaping trout, Or howl of wolf in predatory scout.

A universal calm was in the air,

No earthly plaint or human sigh was there.

A HUNTING SCENE AMONG THE ROCKIES.

Stretched on the sward, beside a mountain lake I view a scene delightful to the eye.

Gazing, fresh beauties grace the lovely scene, The tranquil lake, without a ripple's curl. It sweeps away to distant rocky cliffs

That hem the snow fields, end in Giant peak: Its shores are circled by unbroken chain

Of somber pine woods, and the jutting points Of wooded spaces. thick with willows fring'd. Seclusion reigns here with its wondrous charms. And yet the loneliness oppresses not.

For dumb friends break the scene's monotony ; Where busy beaver labors at his dam,

Or swimming furrows the pellucid lake :

The deer comes down to taste the limpid wave. And wary others creep along the shore,

A flight of wild geese from some Northern realm Drop on the wave, and with a sudden plash Startle the beavers and the blue wing'd teal That have been circling, diving in the bay. Night closes round, so forth to camp I hie, And as I cross the open upland stretch,

Dark forms of deer and elk flit thro' the gloom. Or grizzly bears bent on nocturnal raid. The outline of far peak is landmark clear,

The guiding north star leads me through the woods, Across steep gulches, and by yawning depths Of canyons—safe as beaten trail.

Those somber woods so silent. seen afar, Now as I enter are alive with sound ;

A wapiti emits his plaintive cry,

Standing at gaze. then leaps in headlong flight, A dusky owl repeats his weirdly hoot ;

But the wild realm of nature bath no sound So savage as the lion puma's wail ;

You shudder as it echoes thro' the dusk. A sound so like a piteous human cry,

Fiercer than coyote's shriek, hyena's howl! Our camp beheld from dim recess of shade Bathed with bright light has picturesque effect Nought there to hint of civilized life.

No tent, no couch, no luxuries displayed, Only a hunter's camp, and slaughtered game. No scene more lovely to a hunter's gaze, The world no brighter paradise displays.

THE BLACK BEAR *(Ursus Americanus.)*

The great black bear hath wide-extended range

O'er every region in these banded States ;

In North. in South, in East and Western realms,

It feeds, it prowls. in Winter hibernates. He that would hunt their numbers infinite Must cross Missouri, scale the Rocky Mounts. And riot there in sports beyond compare.

Amid those craggy glooms and pouring founts ; For nowhere in the world is nobler game To crown his efforts with a hunter's fame. In all areas 'tween that mountain chain

And the far waters of Pacific shore, All game indigenous to this Continent

Abounds and ranges the wide region o'er. The grizzly, cinnamon and dusky bear,

Wolves, cougars, foxes and fleet-footed deer Are there to tempt the ardent hunter's search, To dare, to vanish from his bold career.

He must evade the mountain fastnesses,

Explore dense forests and far-spreading plains. The treeless plateaus and the caverns grim, For each a world of faunal life contains Unrival'd in their plenitude of game.

Save in thick jungles of the India's land. Or sunless forests of the Afric world,

Swept by great rivers, crown'd with mountains grand.

The black bear is of sluggish, solitary mood, Prowls in the densest cloisters of each space, Dozing and sleeping at his slothful ease,

Harmless to man and the wild creature race. Its food it seeks where shrubberies grow profuse, Wild berries, grapes and fruits of luscious taste ; Where trampled bush and leaf-stripp'd twigs betray The haunts of those grim creatures of the waste.

Wild animals of size they ne'er attack,

Save when by hungry torments they are press'd. Content on honies, and wild berries fare,

Content to slumber in untroubled rest.

In Southern States where they innumerous roam, In great plantations where they so abound, A bear-hunt is a gala festival,

Pursued by mounted riders and the hounds. 'Tis like a wolf-drive over Russian steppes, Or boar-hunt in the forests of Ardennes,

Where the bold horsemen. arm'd with gun and spear,

Surround their victims in the woods and fens. Great packs of hounds the hunters oft employ,

Hounds lithe and active and of dauntless race, Endow'd with scent acute and tireless speed,

Tracking and yelping in unerring chase. For, keen of scent. and watchful in the ear,

The bear alarm'd is wary of pursuit,

And long ere hunter and the hounds draw near, It vanishes from sight on hurrying foot.

HAUNTS OF WILD GAME.

HUNTING THE GRIZZLY BEAR.

Ursus Hortbt'lis—the grizzly bear

Hath range from Mexico to Canadian realm, From Rocky Mountains to Pacific seas, And ever will the mightiest foe o'crwhelm. Whether in forest or on granite height The conflict rages. the relentless fight. In size. in strength, ferocity supreme, It is the monarch of all animal life ; E'en man himself oft yieldeth to its sway, Shrinks from encounter in the fearful strife. Men claim the lion as the desert's king, Yet the great grizzly is the lion's peer, For grizzly, wounded. would its foe pursue, But *leo* hurt would pause in its career. He is the bear of mountain fastnesses.

As the black bear has home in wood and plain, Yet oft the grizzly roams where food is found, Whether on shrubby plain, or wood-domain. 'Tis denizen of all States in farthest West, It slays the bison by Montana's founts. Its muffled roar disturbs Nevada's wilds, Its sway prevails o'er the Wind-River mounts, Its home is made 'mid craggy cliffs and peaks, Where Mountain-goat and Big-horn sheep abide, And there in dark ravine and canyon grim They prowl they ravage, with their mighty stride. The eagle and the vulture wheel above, But no life else their domains may invade, Save when at times the daring hunter comes With deadly rifle and the bowie-blade. No fear of mortal art, or human power, Hath this grand monster in his wild retreat, For arm'd with fangs and claws like sabre keen, He dreads no valorous assaults to meet. Its taloned paw, its massive jaw will rend The lordly bison at one trenchant blow And the swart Indian. with his shaft and spear. Shrinks from the presence of such dangerous foe, And yet no prouder trophy he may wear

Than necklace of the claws of grizzly bear. In winter's frozen time it hibernates,
Yet then, at limes. he roams the waste for food. Then wild with hunger,
desperate in rage 'Tis death to meet him in his savage mood;
For then with hoarse and drum-like roar he strides, With voice like giants of a fairy
tale
He makes the charge. and woe betide the man, Save for escape some tall tree
may avail: For the grand brute, with courage so sublime, May ne'er with clumsy
limbs the branches climb

THE FRONTIER HUNTER.

By the river's reedy margin
He hath met and slain the bear, And the brindled wolf is dying
In his forest-girdled lair.
Ere the sunset gilds the mountain,
To his but he turns again,
And his panting steed is laden
With the trophies of the slain.
When the golden woods Autumnal.
Glow with all their royal dyes, And the roseate flush of dawning
Crimsons the celestial skies,
Then thro' forests dim the hunter
Follows far his manly toil. Grapples with the grizzly monster.
Daring all things for the spoil. From his cabin in the mountain
Forth he spurs on flying steed, Over prairies far extending,
Grassy swamps and tangled weed ; Fast and far from dawn till evening.
Fast and far he tracks the deer. Till the noble antler'd monarch
Fails and falters in career. Ah, it is a royal pastime !
Ah. it is a gallant life!
Full of hardship, toil and peril,
Stirring as a   battle strife.
He   hath no   delight in riches,
No consuming thirst for gold ;
He, the daring, stout frontiersman,
He the hunter keen and bold.

THE LAST BUFFALO.

Last of his royal race!

He wanders lonely, o'er the trackless waste, Pausing the rolling river's tide to taste,

In the broad desert space.

Gone is that multitude,

That rang'd the grassy, limitless domain, Cropping the sumptuous herbage of the plain,

Their sweet, luxuriant food.

Great monarch of the field!

His shaggy head moved grandly at the front, Triumphant ever in the battle's front,

Scorning to fly or yield.

By Alleghany's chain,

Where the gray summits of the mountains pile, In the green vales 'neath rocky Mount's defile,

The bisons rang'd each plain.

Years since. long-vanish'd years, These giant herds swept o'er the pastures wide.

By Mississippi's shore, Missouri's tide,

Speeding their grand careers.

What terrors they had known ! When rag'd o'er prairies the consuming fire.

When wood and plain, one vast funereal pyre,

With grassy blaze were strown I

Swift the wild cattle fled,

When flam'd afar red Conflagration's sword, Speeding to lakelet marge or river ford,

In tumults dread.

How frantic was their speed,

When Indian tribesmen came with bloody hand. The Blackfoot warriors and the Sioux band,

On galloping, desert steed!

How frantic was the race, While pitiless the whistling arrows sped,

The lassos thrown, the spears with carnage red,

In fierce, relentless chase I

How terrible their lot,

When the train'd soldier from some frontier post With deadly rifle charg'd the flying host With sabre and with shot I

Those great herds pass'd away !

Like leaves autumnal scatter'd o'er the plains Not a poor remnant of them here remains,

In plain or forest-way.

Crippled and daz'd, alone,

Staggering and reeling, bleeding at each pore. Last of his race, a sovereign now no more, He gasps his dying moan!

THE ELK OR WAPITI *(Cervus Canadensis).*

The elk, the noblest creature of the waste

Since the Creation dawn has swept the wild, Ranging the wilderness and prairie plains.

The forest regions—Nature's fleetest child. Where flowery grasses spread their spacious sheet.

Roaming in upland meads and upland slopes, They cropped in freedom the luxurious feast,

Swifter than deer or bounding antelopes. In long-past years, ere emigration pour'd

The settlers, hunters, trappers o er the West, Beyond the Rocky Mountains was their home,

Their haunts, their unmolested place of rest

They rang'd in countless herds Montana's realm,

Wyoming. Utah and far Idaho,

Columbia's wilds and Colorado parks,

Ere came their persecuting white men foe.

This royal ranger, with his lithe, strong frame.

Its branching antlers, its supremest speed, Its proud, its graceful, its defiant mien,

Its wondrous stride, defying racing steed, Was e'er superbest feature of the plain,

Thrilling with ardor sportsman's heart and brain ! In Summer heats he is but thin and week.

But Autumn finds him most robust in frame. Grac'd with full antlers, towering o'r his head,

He roams the forest, grandest of all game

Majestic, ready, like a knight of old.

To meet each rival that would dare the strife. He proudly stamps, and with defiance stares On any foe, save man, that threatens life. After each conquest, matchless is his pace O'er hill and dale and thro' the forest space !

He fears no combat with assailing beast, Save with the grizzly bear, so vast in size ; E'en the black bear. so cruel with his jaws, He grapples in the conflict till one dies He pierces it with antlers sharp and strong, And with mad charges gores it till it fail, Stamps the black carcass, gazing all around To note if other victim might assail

Then, triumphant, stalks glorious from the fray, Slow vanishing in swamp or forest gray. But when an Indian taint infects the air,

And the red tribemen fierce around him sweep, Spurring their frantic steeds in wide career, Swinging their lariats as they onward leap, Whooping their war-cries, while they poise the spear, And shoot the arrows from the bended bow, Then the great elks, with heads erected high, Stare for a moment on the yelling troop, And with consummate speed tumultuous fly.

THE ANTELOPE.

Brave hunters of the boundless West, Path-openers to Pacific shore.

Oft meet the bounding antelope Careering the vast prairies o'er ;

And oft the daring hunter bands, Far toiling thro' the Afric woods

Met jaguars, blessboks, antelopes

Amid those savage solitudes.

Where sweeps th' immeasurable plain, O'er undulating pastures green, Or oft by rocky ridge and cliff,

With dark ravine and chasms between,

And where the waving, tender grass O'erspreads the mountain's lonely pass,

The antelopes in browsing herds Innumerous, in wild freedom rove,

Cropping the verdurous herbage sweet,

Or budding shrubbery of the grove.

So shy, that men almost in vain, May seek to ambush their retreat ; So swift, that nimblest steed may fail

To o'er take the herds so wondrous fleet

Yet stratagem and Indian wile

The timorous game to death beguile. The savage, hidden 'neath some bush Whose leafy clumps the prairies dot, Shakes the green foliage and attracts The cheated prey within his shot ; And oft the warlike Shoshonee, Or Mandan   hunters stark and grim, Circle the herds on coursers swift Fleet   as   the birds the air that skim. Then charging with impetuous speed, With brandished'spear and bended bow, Sounding their fierce. terrific yell. They lay the panting victim low.

The wild wolf of the wilderness

Gaunt, gray and famishing

With loping stride and creeping gait

Surrounds them in concentric ring, And with quick leap the quarry gains, Tearing with fangs their bleeding veins, Till scarcely there remains a bone, Uncrushed, amid the grasses strown.

MULE-DEER *(Cariacus Macrotis).*
In the long-vanish'd years, this continent,
So vast extended from the sea to sea,
Water'd by rivers of majestic course,
Encrown'd with mountains of sublimityShadow'd by forests of supreme extent,
Inlaid with valleys rich with grasses green,
The wild game fill'd the woods, the boundless plains. Their flocks, their herds enlivening each scene, But now from those old haunts they disappear, Though Indian shafts made little havoc there.
Yet when the white-men settlers and the hunters
came,
Vast devastation thinn'd the wild game's lair. The herds of buffalo that rang'd the plains, The moose, the elk, the antelope, mule-deer.
That brows'd the grass of prairies and the mounts, Hunted and slaughter'd, gradual disappear So, too, the wild fowl and the birds of song No longer gather in such countless throng.
The mule-deer roams a realm of vast areas, 'Twixt
Dakota, Nebraska and the Cascade Range. A deer of mountain heights and rough plateau. Yet haunt the pastures of the foot-hills low ; Its favorite haunts are summits of the mounts. Where free from harm a life secure is found, Seeking their timber shelter in the day,
But at the eve, frequenting open ground,
Feeding on herbage that luxuriant grows.
Kept sweet and tender by the melting snows.
In such retreats where wolves may ne'er molest. They, watchful, scrutinize the rocky scene,

Though weak of sight their scent is most acute, Cautious forever of their foes' pursuit,

He that would stalk them must in silence move, For their keen nostrils would a scent betray, Then quick to hear a faint sound would alarm, And swift in flight they vanish far away. Whistling, careering through the lonely woods, The female cries ; the snortings of the male Give life and animation to the scene, Pleasing to hunters on the eager trail ; And if fire-hunting in the glooms of night, He oftimes slays the stately stag and doe, For then attracted by lamp-blaze or torch, They fall an easy victim to the foe.

Not oft in Far West are they chased by hounds, Due to the nature of their rocky home, Their way of dashing to the mountain peaks, Hiding in gulches where they safely roam, For there the scent is lost in stony ground, Defying the pursuit of baffled hound. 'Tis best to hunt when early winter snows Force them to seek the foot-hills for their food, For then they fly not to the craggy steeps, Slow to forsake the coverts of the wood.

MOUNTAIN–SHEEP HUNTING.

These creatures wild have their lone haunts, Only in mountain regions of remotest West ; 'Mid many-pointed crests of soaring mounts, These nimble rovers love to dwell and find

Their dainty food in tender grassy growth: Free from all cares save hunters' daring quest. No game is of such difficult approach, For 'tis of keen scent, and vigilant,

Watching the country from some airy height.

He that would hunt them must be strong and brave For the pursuit must lead in savage scenes, Thro' stony grounds well nigh impassible, Whose towering altitudes and craggy steeps Make the ascent as rough as Alpine peaks.

Though its lone habitats are rugged hills, Yet it will thrive in less mountainous realms If there be rocky cliffs and dark ravines, Where it can refuge seek from ruthless foes. When the flocks migrate to some pastures new, There sentries scrutinize the regions round ; If unalarmed the whole flock feeds at will, There to seek shelter 'mid the pines and firs, And shelves of rocks and sombre canyons deep. Where foes may not unseen invade the haunts.

Whene'er their sentinels view sly approach Of dangerous object, they sound loud alarm: Then the whole column dash for loftiest ridge, And never pause in chasm and crag ; So when disturbed they show intensest fear, And dash for higher pinnacles and mounts. Vaulting from crag to crag, leaping o'er chasms, Plunging adown steep precipices,

Nor pause until assured of safe retreat ; For their great horns are so elastic formed, That falling on them they can safe rebound.

The lambs are dropped in early Spring-time months 'Mid low foot-hills, and when the young grow strong. The dams work gradual in an upward course

'Till they reach snow-line ; there they all remain,

Feeding on succulent herbage of the place ; And linger there till lambs are fully grown, Then scour the hill-sides reveling in the sweets, The freedom of delights in mountain homes.

The   hunter's time to seek them is at morn,

        When the flocks feed or seek some water-course ; Then it is best to stalk or still-hunt up the wind, Seeking an ambush in eack rock and shrub, Creeping with noiseless step, for Big Horn ears Are keen as eyes, forever on alert:

Far up, at windward recesses,

Hidden in ambush by the sheltering rocks A portion of the hunters take their stand And slay the game as they go rushing past.

ROCKY MOUNTAIN GOAT.

Few are the bold frontiersmen,
Who come those mountain realms to dare. To chase the wild flocks of the cliff. Or grapple with the grizzly bear, Amid those savage solitudes,
A desolate and drear domain,
Where rocky ridge and granite peak,
Majestic soar above the plain ;
No tree may live. no plant may grow. No flower the rigid year survive, No browsing drove, no cropping herd, Among those barren pastures thrive, Only those climbing flocks abound, And brindled wolf and bear are found.
The Mandan and the Shosonee,
All armed for battle or the chase, Come with the rifle and the bow, Invading each wide mountain place ; They watch, they lurk in dark defile.
Or where the splintered summits soar, And when the trophy horn is won Turn gladly to the plains once more.
At times to such dim solitude
Come trapper and frontiersman rude, And then for days the cliffs resound, With gun report and hunter's cheer, With baying of pursuing hound, And gallop down recesses drear; There, then, o'er granite ridge and peak, By gorge and gulch and mossy rock, The hunters clamber, plunge or cling. Pursuing the fleet mountain   flock, And at each day-close, spent with toil Return home laden with   the   spoil.

COUGAR *(Fefis Concola).*

The cougar, a fierce creature of the Rocky Mounts. Roams afar thro' forest wilderness ;

With its shrill screamings thrills the very soul Of lonely wanderer in those sunless shades. Though not a dangerous foe till brought to bay, 'Tis fearful terror on the forest-way.

When startled on the ground, the cougar leaps For bushy thicket or for lofty tree.

Whence on some branch its purring cries are heard. Fearful of men. it yet assaults the bear,

Or brindled, howling wolf in lonely lair.

The hunters oft' amid Sierra Mounts

Pitch their lone camps within some green retreat, Before some crystal tarn, in valley hid,

Gay with wild flowers, verdurous with tall grass, Where granite crags like sentinels arise.

And tangled tropics weave shady screen,

And here they oft the lurking cougar meet. And slay the monster in his dense retreat.

So secret, cautious, far from haunts of men, 'Tis rarely met save in recesses green ;

But in the winter they forsake those haunts To prowl around the farmers' settlements,

And on the sheep and cattle make sad raids. Cruel, they slay, yet scarce devour their prey, Killing in willful rage, though gorg'd with food; And so sheep-raisers hunt them to the death, With rifle, strychnine, or avenging knife.

The zealous hunters oft strew tempting bait, And hidden, wait the cougar's slow approach, There late at night they patiently lie hid,

Where no sound breaks the stillness of the glooms, Save fitful hootings of the ghostly owl,

Or plaintive call of the lonely whippoorwill. Or croak of frog, or the tree-locust's whirr, Where all is darkness save the firefly lamps, Illuminating all the shadows of the night.

Nor vain his vigil—for the cougar's scream Is heard at last, and the swift builet kills.

Other wild members of the feline race Roam thro' the regions of the far Southwest, But none save jaguar, so large and fierce, As this fierce cougar of the wilderness. The ocelot. eyre and the prowling lynx, Are all found south along Pacific coasts.

GREAT GRAY WOLF *(Canis Latrans)*.
Wolves range innumerous the great Northwest, And chief of all those prowlers is the Gray; This monster finds in various realms a home, Now scouring in vast herds the level plains, Finding no shelter in that grassy space; Anon again they haunt the forest depths, Secure in mazes of the wilderness;
Anon they haunt the soaring mountain crags, Or o'er the treeless plateaus range at will, Where bushy shelter is infrequent found,
And there make burrows 'neath the clayey banks, Or choose a lair among the open cliffs. The White wolf seeks a Northern habitat, While further south the gray wolves find a haunt, While the Black wolf seeks southern Oregon, And all areas south of Rocky Mounts.
Large. gaunt and fierce, it seems a dangerous foe, Yet 'tis a coward, ever prompt to flee. When strong in numbers the collected pack Will dread encounter with an Indian cur. And when o'ertaken they will pause and snarl And seek escape from such inferior foe. When wolves, in droves, large animals pursue, Such as the bison or the bulky elk,
They scatter in small flocks around the route The quarry takes, and so pull down their game. When a strong pack pursues a fleeing prey,
The victims yield before such strength and speed, They constant follow herds of antelope, Or buffaloes, browsing the vast grassy plains, Prowling around them in their devious route.

E'en in the wintry regions of the North, They prey insatiate on a lesser game, Badger and fox, the prairie dog and hare, And when with hunger stung, in wintry times They prowl ardund the farmers' homes for spoil.

Great is the sport to hunt those wolfish herds. With blast of horn and howling cries of hounds, And when the mounted Indian tribes pursue. They form a circle round the fleeing pack And to a centre drive them to their death.

So vast the numbers of these savage wolves,

So vast the hunting grounds o'er treeless plains That in the future years the grand wolf-hunt, Must prove the noblest pastime of the chase.

PRAIRIE WOLF, OR COYOTE *(Canis Lames).*

The howling serenades, the yelping screams, Of the wild coyotes of the boundless plains Are heard from Canada to Mexic realms,

From Northern mount to Southern hot domains. Prowling at night, their dismal outcries warn The settlers, that no Indian foes are near; But when these cease, frontiersmen take alarm, And arm to meet the tribesmen's fierce career.

Wide o'er Columbian plains their packs abound. Beyond the Cascade Range ; for there are spread Free feasts of sage hare and the badger game. And thick on shores are strewn the salmon dead. Timid, they fly at near approach of man

And from the deer-hounds in their keen pursuit, From Indian mustangs, when the savage tribes Cast the long lariat, or their arrows shoot. Those riders, in their headlong spurt of speed,

Stirr'd by the flute-like music of the hound,

May soon o'ertake them. but there's dangerous fall When the swift horse may trip o'er rocky ground In hole of prairie dog or squirrel mound.

White hunters, ranging the broad prairie plains, Pitching the camp at foot of mountain height,

Are charm'd 'mid scenes where Nature reigns supreme,
'Mid the great forests and by streamlets bright. They gaze o'er vales whose breaths of sweetest air Blow o'er grass billows on from crest to crest, Or made soft sighing through the willow bush, Whose leaflets were by gliding streams carest ; Where voices of the night fill'd all the plain—The night hawk, flitting on its dusky wings, And the weird baying of the coyote packs, Now far, now near, in fitful murmurings.

Slow pass'd the night ; anon the gates of dawn Swept back and the young day came dancing out, And far o'er mountain peaks the breeze dispers'd The silvery mist-wreaths in dissolving rout ; Abroad came creatures of the earth and air, And all was life and motion o'er the earth ; Yet, far below, green valleys were asleep :

No light had touch'd, no breeze the foliage stirr'd, The brook slipt on in shadow, without sound, Nor yet was heard the song of early bird.

From some green slope a solitary cliff

Rear'd its proud crest above the valleys low, While on horizon a long, glimmering file

Of craggy peaks and silvery summits glow, All bath'd in purple tints and roseate hues, The hues that Sierra Madre soft suffuse !

Here groups of scarlet cacti-blossoms gleam'd, 'heath mesquit bushes, each a
flaming ball, While waxen flowerets, coral or
deep red, Bloom'd 'neath the clusters of amolias

tall. Years since, one Winter day, we join'd a group Of hunters mustered on a wolf-hunt raid ;

Thro' deep-heap'd snows our sledges plow'd their way,

O'er open prairies, or thro' bushy glade.

In circling, narrowing rings our hunters press*d, Beating loud drum and sounding horn and trump ; Then, all concentrated in one open vale.

We drove the game from grass and thicket-clump. Then hounds were loos'd to massacre the prey

For rifles were forbid in such close fray ;
So, then, we slew with axe and club and spear, The captur'd wolves, the foxes and the deer.

AFRICAN HUNTERS AND EXPLORERS.
Brave men from distant. European land,
Explorers seeking sources of the Nile,
Have zealously pierced each boundless wilderness. Scaled mountain summits, dashed thro' dark defile ;
They marched thro' sunless deserts where the sands Heaped their white dunes like billows of the main: They traversed deserts where great caravans Toiled o'er the herbless waste, the arid plain; They penetrated Blooms of forests wild,
Pressed thro' morasses. pestilential swamps, And by Nyanza's unexplored expanse,
Pitched on its grassy banks their midnight camps.
They sought at Albert Lake a needful rest. Where sweet mimosas and palmyras grew, Resting luxurious 'neath acacia shades.
Where tropic plants their brilliant blossoms strew.
There journeyed fearless Clapperton and Grant, Burton and Baker, Du Chaillu and Park, Brave Gordon Cumming and grand Livingstone, Saved by our Stanley in those regions dark ; These fearless. hostile native tribes they met, Who ruthless all their venturous paths waylaid. Hovering around their guarded camps at night, Wielding the assagai and bloody blade.
Amid great storms of hurricane and rain, Tormented by malarious disease,
Hungry and thirsting still they journeyed on,
Enjoying rest beneath great forest trees.
In boundless plains they sought the roving herds, The gnu, the antelope, the tawny deer,
They slew the lion amid ravines grim,

Leopard and panther. in their fierce career ; The fleeing blesbok and the pallah wild, And oft rhinoceros by stagnant pool.

The giraffe or unwieldly elephant
Or quagga bathing in some fountain pool.

Dark frowned the woods upon their dangerous way ! Where Nature spread a desolate expanse, Where riotous, broad rivers barr d their route,

In wilds where sunbeam never cast a glance. So dense the shades in those primeval woods

That scarce they caught the beam of day ;

No flowery dells, no meadews fresh and green

No grassy turf with its perennial bloom

To charm the sight and sanctify the scene !

Yet onward still in perilous advance, Fearless of savage beast or lurking foes,

These brave invaders of the wilderness

Press'd on triumphant to the journey's close !

WILD GAME OF AFRICA.

Far had intrepid Stanley urg'd his way,

O'er arid deserts, over grassy plains,

Struggling thro' tangled. pestilential swamps. Where vene mous serpents coil'd their spotted folds. Crossing the White Nile and the Congo's breadth, Tumultuous streams, along whose reedy banks Huge crocodiles up threw their scaly snouts. The black rhinoceros wallow'd in the tide, Hippopotamus roll'd his dusky bulk,

And the great elephant. swinging high his trunk, With flapping ears, resorted there to drink ;

All creatures of the wild swarm'd round his way, Quaggas and pallahs, antelope· and gnu,

The tusked boar, the tall giraffe. whose head Stretch'd high to crop the sweet acacia leaves, The striped zebra and the dusk harte-beest. The nimble spring-bok, dark with tawny hide, All trampled there to lap the rushing wave • And lave in tropic heats their panting sides.

In his brave path he skirted craggy cliffs, Ruvenzori's Mount, a mountain world!
Ridge over ridge. peak soaring over peak. Caverns, dark ravines, jutting cones,
High o'er some knoll his eye o'erlooked the scene. Panorama grand, a paradise of green!
Beneath, broad valleys stretch'd their verdurous space,
Lac'd with the sparkling stream or purple lake, Shadow'd by palm tree or primeval oak.
Far in blue distance swept a boundless range Of rolling mountains, vitrified like waves
Not one bare spot nor arid dune of sand
To mar the glory of this lovely land!
Oft by some darkling stream, at dead of night, In bushy ambush, 'mid papyrus reeds,
The daring hunter, with his rifle-gun,
Would with a throbbing heart await the game. Anon some roving deer would meet its fate, Anon a lion, scenting taint of blood,
Would come with shaggy mane and monstrous head
To seize his prey—himself a victim, too :
Anon a heavy tread would crush the ground, When twigs would crack, trees topple as he came Anon his giant bulk be dimly seen,
Anon his twisting trunk would dip the wave, And spouted fountains lave his heated flanks, Then would the rifle pour its blazing death, And huge leviathan would sink in gore!
Here was the hunter's paradise of sport, Endless successes 'gainst the noble game !
Wondrous his triumphs, and great perils past. Lent thrill'd excitement to the hero's heart. He knew the perilous crisis of the hour. Knew that his life he ventur'd on the cast,
Knew that false aim would goad each monster on, Then cruel death would be his certain fate! Yet still he lived—his happy lot to save Devoted Livingstone from Afric grave!

HUNTING THE AFRICAN OSTRICH.

Near the equator, the fierce tribes
From wattled but and herdsman's kraal.
Gather on fleetest steed to hunt The stately ostrich on its trail.
They note its track on desert sand, They hear its guttural, hollow cry
A cry like lion's distant roar,
A warning, as they haste to fly.
The riders spur on striding steed,
While footmen sweep in circles round.
Swinging the slender assagaie, Eager the victims to surround.
By some clear fountain in the waste, Shaded by palm-trees' leafy screen,
The ostrich makes its secret haunt Where spring the water grasses green ;
To browse on grass in such retreat They taste at will the waters sweet.
The mounted tribes, at dawn of day, With slackened pace the prey pursue, As the colossal bird speeds on, Slow-follow'd, yet not lost to view. Oufstripping the pursuing foe,
They pause at times around to glance.
As if defying the pursuit,
They stand awaiting the advance. Anon on rapid flight they speed, Oft pausing in the swift career, While with a gradual approach
The   tribemen move with brandish'd spear.
So,   while   the heat is not intense, The ostrich shows superior speed, But as the noonday heats prevail, Fatigued, it yields to swifter steed. And then the hunters, spurring fast, Rush in and seize the prey at last.
The tribesman with stragetic art. Disguised with feathers like the game,

Deceiving the unwary bird, Destroy it with the arrow's aim. They imitate with cunning skill, Seeming to browse on grass the while, Then when in bow-shot of the game, They slay the victims of their guile. Oftimes the ostrich male will chase This strange deceiver of his race ; Who drops disguise and flees amain, Detected culprit in the chase.

Beauty and youth in lordly hall,

Where diamonds flash and rubies shine. Delight to wear the ostrich plumes,

On brows where sparkling wreaths entwine. The pearls, the gems are fair to see, But none more fair than tiara That once the hapless ostrich wore, In Afric regions, far away.

HUNTING THE GIRAFFE.

In Central Africa the giraffe tribes

Have chosen haunts o'er all the grassy plains, And 'mid the forest glooms they love to roam. Timid in danger, at approach of men Spurring their panting horses in mad race, They speed away in frantic gallopings, Defying the swift steed and native spear. A British hunter in that forest realm, Who first beheld this giant of the wilds,

Gazed with amazement at its wondrous height, And, fired with sportsman's zeal, forgot all else, Pain and fatigue, and perils of the waste, In presence of such grand, stupendous game.

They range in dense, impenetrable woods, Feeding on tropic plants of lavish bloom, Where the palmyras lift their verdurous crowns, And sweet mimosas and the mopant thrive, And where acacias wave their banners green. 'Tis there the stately camelopards dwell, Secure in refuges of sylvan shades.

Oft where the open plains extend their space, They mix with herds of blessbok and the gnu. The pallahs. quaggas and fleet antelope ;
And when the tribal savages pursue,
They lead the flight of th' escaping game.
Oft they forsake the sheltering depths of groves To browse on shrubberies that fringe the plains. And here the hunters, with their native scouts, Surround in circles the beleaguer'd game,
They swing their rifles, while the brandish'd spears Of the swart tribesmen terrify the herds ;
Then comes a general panic o'er the plains.
A matchless speed—then gunshot and the death ! Peaceful and timid, ever prompt to fly,
How strange the gait of this far-striding game ! With neck outstretch'd and head sway'd to and fro. They clumsily roll on with wondrous speed, Sweeping with mighty leaps o'er marsh and bog. Bursting through bushy coverts of the waste. Though quick to flee, yet oft, when brought to bay. They will with striking hoofs their foes o'erthrow. When a grim lion springs upon its back,
Plunging its claws, and gnawing the tall neck ; Then lion and giraffe, with life-blood dyed. Will sink to earth, expiring side by side!

HUNTING THE N JENA-GORILLA.

In sunless forests, in dense thicket glades,

The Afric wild beasts devasting roam, And here in fastness of dim wilderness

The fierce gorilla makes his savage home. He is the king, the sovereign of the waste :

No living creature dare his haunts molest ; The *gnu,* the pallah and the hartebeest fly

From his approach at coverts of his rest. E'en the grim lion turns aside in dread,

The spotted leopard vanishes in fear,

And the huge elephant mighty in his strength,

Flies from such foe in hurricane career.

The native kraalmen of those tangled wilds,

Ne'er dared to meet this terror of the woods. Vain were their arrows and their assegais.

Vain the assaults of swarming multitudes.

Yet when brave hunters from the Northern shores

Came with their deadlier weapons in the hand. The volleying shot, the fatal bullet flew,

Then the fierce gorilla died, a victim grand ! A hunter tells how 'mid thick sugar-canes,

He first beheld the spoor of this great beast :

        Thrill'd high his heart to meet there face to face

        This monster of the forests, at his feast. Oft had he heard

of this ferocious king,

To civilized mankind so long unknown,

So famed for cunning, courage and brute strength,

A royal sovereign on his desert throne. Though bright the day, the hunter and his train

Charg'd thro' the brushwoods sombre with their

shade.

Sudden rose the gorilla's barking roar

As the great beast sprang from a bushy glade, Sudden he paused. and fearless met his gaze,

With brandished arms and bold erected head, With fiercely glaring *eye* and fiendish face,

Like nightmare vision, filling heart with dread!

Frantic he beat with claws his tawny breast,

That like a muffled drum resounded loud, Then a sharp bark: and then a hollow roar, Like rolling thunder from a temptest cloud. There as he stood his eyes flash'd fiercest fire. The crested hair twitch'd o'er his sable brow His gnashing fangs gleamed terrible with ire, He seem'd like creature of a midnight dream, Half man, half beast, a hideous sprite of hell, Such as old painters pictur'd in their art. The shapes that in infernal regions dwell. When quick repeating his unearthly roar, The bullet sped, the monster's life was o'er!

ROAR OF THE AFRICAN LION.

This noble monarch of the Afric waste Meets with no rival to contest his reign, With his surpassing strength and agile stride He can o'ercome each creature of the plain. He dashes to the earth the tall giraffe

Who towers above the summits of the woods; He tracks the herds of shaggy buffaloes, And slays the bull in solitudes ;

He preys on nimble flocks of antelopes, The pallah, oryx, quagga and wild-beest. O'ertakes the blesbok in its swiftest flight, On zebra and the eland makes his feast.

How grand. how thunderous his savage roar ! First he emits a dull, far-echoing moan

That ends at times with faintly-whispered sighs, At other times he startles all the herds

With deep-toned roar and wild, tempestuous cries That sudden sink away in muffled tone, Like distant thunder fading in the skies.

His roar is loudest in cold, frosty nights

When two troops meet beside a fountain's flow ; Then each troop sounds a bold, defiant roar, Each seeking to out-roar the rival foe. Those grand, nocturnal concerts fill the waste With universal terror, yet they thrill,

With transport the brave hunter's fearless heart,

Who lies there close ambush'd, resolute to kill ; A hunter in the glooms of forests hid, In the dead hour of midnight, all alone ; Ensconced in thicket at the fountain's edge, Listing the awful roar, or hollow moan.

The lions roar incessant in the night,

Their sighing moans beginning with the shades Of evening ; gather in the forest depths, Sounding their warnings in the dim arcades Thro' all the day they rest concealed in shade Of gloomy forests on some mountain side, Loving the jungles or the tangled grass In low-lying shelves or in the valleys wide ;

From thence they stalk, when ends the sunset glow, Intent on nightly prowl for wandering foe, Then in dark night their roar is full of ire, Their eyeballs glowing like two balls of fire.

AFRICAN LION AND OTHER ANIMALS.

Brave hunters from far European realms, Have wide explored the unknown Afric lands, Skirting great rivers, crossing mountain range. Seeking the source of nameless stream and lake. Where fired with sportsman ardor they pursued. The wild game denizens of wood and plain. The Afric natives arm'd with assagais.

Would fail those agile creatures to destroy; Too swift for them the gambols of the gnu, The onyx, hartebeest or the quagga herds, The blesbok, zebra, or the tall giraffe.

Too fierce for their weak shafts the lion-king, The tapirs huge, arm'd with their ivory tusks, The hippos, panthers.

or the elephant,

The rhinoceros or the buffalo ;

But those white strangers from the foreign land, Arm'd with their deadly rifles would outmatch The fiercest monsters of the Afric land.

Those brave explorers with a valorous zeal The lion-monarch of the wilds would meet,

Would lie in ambush for his shaggy form,

Dashing thro' wastes, or lapping some clear stream. Those hunters found in many a grassy glade The trampled couch where he had made retreat : They sought him at the base of mountain crags, Or in dim vistas of the cork-tree grooves, In woods with mosses and gray lichens draped, 'Mid tangled festoons of lianas green,

Engarlanded with gray ochilla weed;

And o'er the undulating plains would seek, The lordly lion, frantic in career.

There in broad day the lion stands at bay Watching with rage that strange, assailing band, Then shortly turns, and leisurely stalks away, Then with swift leaps he like a greyhound flies, —Too late, too late for quick the bullet strike3! The hunters tell that once they pitch'd their camp In a green valley of the Kandely,

A picturesque and most enchanting spot,

An open glade fring'd with the cotton-woods, Where in its midst meandered a clear brook. On one side stood a red-haired antelope. Near a baobab, gazing at the band,

While gnus and tesbees watch'd them in alarm. Some careless fed, while some in anger gaz'd. Anon a big white rhinoceros pass'd.

With sauntering gait, unmindful of the camp : .Dark-visaged buffaloes group'd beneath the trees, And all seem'd quiet, and no panic reign'd, When sudden with a bound and savage roar, A shaggy lion sprang amid the group ; Then instant came confusion in the place, As all the creatures struggled to escape —When quick a death-shot laid the lion low I

WHITE POLAR BEAR.

In the far North where Arctic vigors reign Man penetrates with awe the dreary scene, Lured by weird glooms of the sunless year. In silences of solitudes serene.

Like a vast ocean. waveless, frigid, while, Faint-lighted by the crescent moonbeams' glance, Or by blue streams of auroral light.

The land stretch'd endless in its dim expanse. There was no light or warmth to cheer the waste, While the faint radiance of moon or star Ting'd like a stormy sunset the deep snows, Causing a mirage floating high and far. Lamented Franklin here explorings made, And with his seamen perish'd in the snow, Where Hall. Kane. Peary, Greeley, gallant men, Sought the North Pole far as mankind could go !

There 'mid grand icebergs slipping from the cliffs Or on the drifting floes that chok'd the tide, Gigantic Polar bears, so grim and gaunt,

In solitary majesty abide.

Their haunt is some vast cave with icy walls, Where bright stalactics glisten overhead.

And pendent icicles drop splinter'd points.

Like pearly spars in grottoes overspread,

They live secluded thro' inclement year,

All undisturb'd by step of human foe,

Save when at times, arm'd with the deadly lance. Invading their retreats comes Esquimaux.

At times when whale-ships anchor by the shore, And seamen cut the blubber from the whale, The prowling bear-herds gather to the feast, And with wild rush the mariners assail.

Little of life across these wastes is seen,

Save where the gull and auk go screaming by, Or duck or loon or white-wined ptarmigan Startle the silence with discordant cry, Or musk ox or the walrus by the shore For finny spoil the frozen space explore.

CAMPS AND CAMPING.

THE HUNTERS' CAMP.

Here on the craggy ridges and gray peaks
The hunters gazed far o'er the outspread land ; Far in the blue horizon rose the cones
And splinter'd pinnacles, supremely grand ; Beneath, great rivers dwindled into brooks,
And swept bright courses thro' the valleys green. Fring'd by thick groves of cottonwood and oak,
Engirdling lakes transparent and serene ;
Fair that broad scene when sunset skies are red
Illuminating forests, plains and streams, Beauteous when night is sprinkled with its stars.
' When showering moonlight casts its tremulous
beams.
Ye may have journey'd wide o'er foreign realms.
Have trod the streets of Paris and of Rome, Gaz'd on the Jungfrau and the snowy Alps,
On Parthenon ruins and St. Peter's dome, Have roam'd the lovely valleys of the Loire,

Have sail'd the Rhine, the Danube and the Nile. The
Thames, the Shannon, Caledonian Tweed,

Watch'd the new day o'er Scottish mountains
smile,
Smile on Ben Nevis and gray Benvenue,
Loch Katrine's mirror, Lomond's waters blue ;
Yet n e'er perhaps ye've view'd the wondrous scenes.
O'er all your native country widely spread, Ne'er gazed on Pike's Peak or Nevada range.
Each blooming valley and each mountain-head; Ne'er seen Niagara, or Missouri's tide,
Or roamed where Mississippi currents glide, Ne'er visited our streams, our forests grand, Our lakes, or wonders of the prairie land.
The hunters' camp! Ah, 'tis not solitude
To be with Nature in her grand domain ;
Ye and your brethren, far from human crowd, Gazing on mount and forest, plain and glen ; The electric lights of cities are afar,
No din of traffic, and no railway jar
Disturb your lives; ye have the sparkling gleams

Of stars and moonshine, with their radiant beams ; The songs of birds, the only sounds *ye* hear, Or plaint of leaves, the hymns of waters clear ; Richer the joys of stream and forest-way.

Than Saratoga, Long Branch or Cape May. At morn throw wide the tent-fly and pass out,

How balmy, then, how sweet the liberal air ! You view the outlines of remotest hills, Touch'd in the East by colorings rich and rare Then bird-songs swell athwart the mountain slopes, A jocund orchestra, with chorus sweet ;

The dawning light fills all the bosom'd vale,

Flooding with blaze each pastoral retreat ;

The new light prints on earth a morning kiss,

The floating clouds are fring'd with lustrous lines, The green trees fluttering, greet the new-born day. The wild flowers twinkle with the pearly dews ; All Nature smiles a welcome to the eye,

In woods, in valleys, in the arching sky.

THE ANGLER IN CAMP.

We cheerfully sit in our camp when the eve

Drops its dim shades over forest' and stream, And reflectingly muse in this region remote,

Pleased with the sound of the wave and its
                         gleam.

We think of far homes with their bustle and din, We scarce realize that there the dark cares, Commotions, distresses, ever prevail,

That ever disturb their great thoroughfares!

Ah, the joy of the sportsman 1 Methinks more and more

The people appreciate all its delights;

They feel that it yields an increase of health,

It charmeth the days, it brightens the nights.

More and more will the sons of traffic and trade

Be attracted to haunts where Nature doth reign. Will be weaned from the false dissipations of life

To enjoy the free sports of river and plain.

So, too, will the angler's, the hunter's, great field

Be enlarged, as the sports more popular grow, And protection and increase of fishes and game Will encourage the sport with high born and low.

Good fishing will then be found nearer home, And so, tastes once formed fair places remote Will be sought, and frequented year after year, And far-away streams become places of note. Then fish as game fish, that now are unknown, Will come into note, be recorded as game ; The carp and the shad will rise to the fly, And the grayling augment the angler's fame: Then will supply forever increase.

And the love for the angling never will cease. Ye that have had experience with rod

Need not be told now of Nature's fair scenes, Of the unbroken lines of grand forest trees,

Of the shadows that sleep on the breast of the

lake,

And their depths that witness festivities.

The joy of taking the bright fish is great, But greater the joy of gazing around,

To glance at the woodlands and waters free, Hear the songs of the birds, the torrent's sound, And all the pleasures that Nature doth yield To the lover of sport in Turf, Farm and Field.

'Tis good to look up, reflecting on Nature's God. To note all His wondrous works of majesty   Wrought in heavens above and earth beneath, And in the watery depths of   the sea.

For he that loves sport loves N ature, too—The skies, and the earth, and the ocean blue.

MUSING AT AN ADIRONDACK LAKE.

Alone at night ! The river black below.

Dark banks in front. the murky woods around. The hollow roar of rushing waterfall, The hoot of owl, the wolf packs distant sound, All make a scene of deepest solitude ; Man is so far off, God so grandly near ;

The wilderness is one great tongue that speaks The human hearts in accents wondrous clear. Not in the desert solitudes of space

Not o'er the seas do we so realize

The Presence that pervades the loneliness, For here the forest temples round us rise And hearts expand in all this wilderness.

A Sabbath day I The skies are robed in gold With purple hues fringed with a pearly sheet The lake sleeps breathless, not a leaf is stirred. Viewing the scenes repose I thought how sweet The sanctity of Sabbath in the mind. That finds a sympathy in vast universe

For on this kind day Nature's pulse seems stilled. The waters ripple with a calmer course The forests rustle with a gentler grace, Birds seem to chant with sweeter melodies. A perfect calm pervades the human heart, And Nature purifies the earth and skies.

By Tupper Lake the trapper finds his spoil, The muskrat holds the busy beaver's home. Where that shrewd architect builds his dam. With tender saplings, a surmounting dome. There, too, he traps the fisher and the mink, The furry otter, sables, a rich prize

Where, too, the hunter drives the dappled deer Hunts him thro' forests as he frantic flies, Then seeks escape by swimming river-tide. Pursued by hounds, tormented till he dies! Here, too, the wild ducks haunt the open lake, The speckled loons their dismal hootings sound. Great eagles o'er the mountain summits soar, The wide-wing'd herons skim the waters rour.d ; The anglers here their spotted victims take By flowing stream or o'er the Tupper Lake.

IN CAMP AT SARANAC LAKE.

Solitude reigns supreme—silence fills my heart I High in the solemn heavens God seems near ; Far off the busy world seems far apart !

Here I abide, forgetting that far world—

That anxious world—while I am happy here;

Here solitude teaches peace, that perfect rest, Where sweeps the wilderness in wild career.

Sin, pride. ambition never enter here.

May human breath ne'er taint this purest air,

But free may forests spread and teach their pure True lessons of the freedom of the woods,

The perfect liberty, the courage to endure. Here with long tassels soar majestic pines,

The sombre hemlocks and the cedars green, Clinging to rocky ledge and granite crag :

Dense cones of spruce arise, a bowery screen. The beech, the birch, the streaked moose-wood grove,

Rise like tall steeples as they upward soar ; A firmament of foliage high above,

Ferns, mosses, vines, all forming a green floor. The landscape round is full of stirring life,

The pendant foliage stirr'd by wandering breeze ; Woodpeckers clutching the rough maple bark, A sable raven floating o'er the trees ;

Ground squirrels gambol o'er a mossy log. And far below the trout leap in the tide,

Ducks rise with splash, herons spread their sail.

Hawks, jays and eagles o'er the woodlands glide. There is a charm in every woodland sound, A perfect peace, with solitude profound ;

There's not a jar the bosom to distress

In this fair Eden of the wilderness.

Ah, let all lovers of the wilderness.

Lovers of Nature, now in league conspire To save from devastation these grand works Threatened by lawless bands with axe and fire; Let these great forests spread their leafy arch To catch the falling rains, the dews, the snows,

That the broad Hudson may maintain its tides, Fed by each tributary stream that flows, So that Fee Park, a national domain.
Shall spread in grandeur over mount and plain !

THE WOODS AND WATERS OF MAINE.

Far in sunset's mellow glory, far in daybreak's rosy bloom,
Fring'd by ocean's stormy surges. belted in by woods of gloom.
Stretch thy sandy. rocky borders, smile thy shores in hill and plain ;
Flower-embroidered, ocean-girdled, green, fair shores of Maine !
Rivers of surpassing beauty from thy hemlock uplands flow;
Androscoggin and Penobscot, Saco chilled with mountain snow.
These from many a darkling ravine, as o'er mossy rocks they leap.
Sparkling, bear their ice-cold tribute to the surges of the deep.
Bays are thine as heaven transparent, starr'd and gem'd with countless isles ;
Quoddy with its emerald inlets, Casco with its dimpled smiles.
O'er them swift the coasting schooners, stately ships their wings expand,
While the smoke-flag of the steamer waves its cloudy, vapory streamer,
Sailing o'er the frothy billow for some European land.
Moosehead Lake in girdling forest spreads afar its azure breast,
Lonely, solitary, silent, slumbering in a drowsy rest ;
Silent, save when o'er the waters. fring'd with pine tree and with fir,

Roars the thrashing winter tempest, or the summer breezes stir.
Years ago, in native Maine land, sought I the deep forest shades,
Wandering far, a musing student, in your bowery arcades.
Shadowy woods of classic Brunswick ! how reposeful to recline
Underneath the sombre hemlocks, or the towering. plumy pine !
College friends were there—dear Longfellow, with the matchless poet's lyre :
Prentice. in the ofter years so famous for his oratoric fire.
Noble forests full of transport to the ardent sportsman's heart,
With their pigeon-flocks and partridge flitting thro' each bushy haunt.
There we view'd the Androscoggin flowing past its verdant shore,
Lingering long by wood and meadow the fair borders to explore ;
View'd the crystal currents flowing, dashing, foamy to the strand ;
View'd the shining fishes darting, tempting spoil for angler's hand ;
View'd the silvery sturgeon leaping, flashing o'er the river's brim,
While the air was vocal ever with the tuneful songbird's hymn !

" I will build me a camp by a cool mountain spring,
Where the trout play at eve and the wood-thrushes sing ; I will roof it with bark ;
and my snug sylvan house Shall be sweet with the fragrance of evergreen
boughs."
-FOREST RUNES.

153

OUR CAMPS IN THE FAR WEST.

Far have we journey'd over barren plains, Where only the wild sage-bush fills the way, Have pass'd Wind river and Shoshone realms. Fording great water-courses in the route ;

Have gazed on peaks crown'd with eternal snow, Fremont and Teton soaring high in air,

And here among the mountains pitch our camp.

Have found wild game abundant in the way, Have slain the bighorn and the wapiti, Track'd the fierce grizzly to his rocky lair. Chased o'er the plains the rushing bison-herd. Follow'd the antelope in frantic chase, And ambush'd elk and deer in wild retreats.

The Alpine scenery is rich with charms, Inlaid with lakelets lovely to behold ;

Oft' o'er their space were seen the tufted-ducks And the wild geese alighting on the lake, Great herds of wapiti and uncouth moose, Wading knee-deep along the shallow shore.

Deep are those lakes so crystal-clear, serene, Above the timber-line engirt with rocks, Hemm'd by Titanic boulders gray and rough. So clear are they, that from o'er-jutting cliff Your gaze may penetrate to deep abyss, While others shallow show their sandy bed.

Some swarm with fish resplendent with their scales. While others yield no sign of living   thing.

No   beaver-sign, no deer-track by the shore ; Yet grand the look of great mountain-tarns. Where whiteman's eye mayhap hath never gaz^{e}d.

Here on this happy-hunting-ground we rest. Where all sights are delightful to the sense

We view vast stretches of the blue-green pines. And deep-green beaver-meadows we have cross'd. Scenes well in contrast with the desert plains.

There is a varied charm in this wild life

So free, so independent. in its round !

Emancipated from all cares of human-kind, Uncheck'd by chains of civilized life.

Here you may roam as free as browsing deer, Here pitch your camp in liberty supreme,

Find sports that charm the sportsman's gay career. The subtle joys to naturalist so dear !

BEYOND THE ROCKY MOUNTAINS.

In long past years the bold frontiersmen-bands, Hunters of deer and elk and bison herds, And trappers seeking their fur-bearing game, Traversed afar the Rocky Mountain range, So that they knew each canon and defile, Each lonely lake, each river of the land. Each great fur company held there their post, Where traders traffick'd with the Indian tribes, Eager for peltries and the bison robes, And ofttimes battling in a stormy fight.

Those mountaineers would scale the steepest cliffs: A hardy race, extravagant of speech. In thought and deed regardless in their ways, Ready for bounteous feast'or deadly, fray. In vain the savages beset their way, In vain the rocks and torrents barred their route. Let but a trace of beaver meet the eye, He scorns all perils and defies all harm. He lov'd to roam the sternest fastnesses, He lov'd to pitch his camp in forest depths, But chief he lov'd to track the flowing stream, Taking the leaping salmon in their course; And chief he lov'd the great Columbia's banks, And the Snake River's picturesque career.

He pitch'd his tent at base of mountain slope, Whose tops were sheeted by eternal snows,

Their white robes dropping in the Winter months , Until they spread a mantle o'er the plains; Great drifts that drove the browsing buffaloes To seek the river borders for their food, There to be slaughtered by relentless foes.

Those hunters roving by Nebraska's banks Were ofttimes ambushed by the warlike Crows, Grim foes, red-painted and array'd for war, Mounted on steeds decked out with trappings wild, Came prancing round them in most gallant style, Whirling in evolutions intricate,

Waving the arms that sparkled in the fight. A picturesque and glittering cavalcade.

CAMPS IN THE TIMBERLINE RANGE.

Glorious it is to roam in this broad ridge, The main divide of this great continent!

Now catching glimpses of the southern slopes, Snow of flashing views of barren peaks, Views of Sierras Shoshone at north. Pleasant it was that region to exchange

For timbered slopes of Big Wind river mounts! Here on this grand divide, three noble streams Take their headwaters on the mountain sides; One, the Wind river, the confluent chief Of the Missouri, to the Atlantic flows; Another streamlet joins Columbia's tides, Merging at last in North Pacific seas, While Colorado, third headwater sends Its tribute to the California gulf;

Such are the mazy creeks, the silvery streams That flow from forests in remotest course.

Fxplorers found 'mid Colorado mounts

Full many a pleasant refuge for their camps, Whose fair surroundings were a fresh delight. From some green swards so idly like in charms Rose straight and massive soaring cotton woods, With trunks of silvery sheen, while festoons green Of vines and creepers, twining garland like. Bound the tree tops, and a bowery shade, In front of camp would sweep a river broad, Its glossy face by twirling eddies swept, Where oft in deeps the limpid waters slept, Great salmon trout would hover 'neath the bank;

A perfect solitude : with not a sound
Of bird or animal the calm to break ;
For wapiti and stately forest elk
And big prong horn were far off on the mounts And grizzly bears were distant in their haunts. Here o'er this brilliant mass of verdure rose The grand titanic Taton, a vast mount,
Up soaring miles away, yet seeming near,
High thrusting its sharp peak above these groves : Clear was the air, deceptive in its light
In these old camps what happy days were passed. What dreamless slumbers in the depth of night! What social greetings by the campfire's blaze. There exploits were rehearsed and songs were
sung
Beneath those shadows of primeval trees, Beneath the starry canopy of night,
How joyous sped each gay eventful day !
As the camp fires illumed the woodland scene, Brightening the solemn shades, the arcades dim, They touched with lurid flames the hemlock boughs
And brown. columnar phalanx of the pines ; So fancy then with spectral
ghost-like wand Would people all the shades with
phantom shapes!

LONG ISLAND BEACH.

The gusty east wind blows amain,

The fog banks settle o'er the watery plain

• Great clouds, like shadows. weigh upon the deep. Or fast, like battle frigate's sweep. 'Til all the curling summits of the foam As whitely o'er the vapory seas they comb,

Fade in the grey immensity of space, 'Til billows in their never-ending race Are blotted from the sight.

Fair blows the eastern breeze! Instant the sunbeam glitters o'er the seas. Aside the hovering shadow drifts, Upward the vapory curtain lifts. Like routed files, like conquer'd ranks Of armies. broken on their flanks. And fleeing madly in retreat Before the pursuer's hurried feet, So fly the dark and rainy shades,-As fast the shining light invades.

Far as the gazing eye can strain The broad, the blue, illimitable main Stretches its vast eternal plain.

To the horizon's edge ;

Across its liquid hills and vales, Far travers'd by the ghostly sails. Across its foamy-crested waves That comb above the watery caves, Across the tumbling breakers tost O'er the low-lying reach of coast. O'er curving cove and limpid bay The bright, rejoicing sunbeams play And flush with soft and roeseate glow

Old   ocean's ebb and flow.

Now sinks the sun behind the hills,

Night with her glooms the landscape fills, Unseen the billows heave and break, Unseen the voyaging vessels take

Their lonesome way in gloom profound

Afar on lonely wanderings bound. Far to the west, Fire Island Light, A spark,
gleams out upon the night ; Far to the east Montauk illumes
With trembling ray the ocean glooms, While near the lanterns of Pon Quogue
Brighten the ocean's hazy fog, TAI deep and dim o'er billow crests The
mantle of the midnight rests.

GREENWOOD LAKE.

Fair lake. so picturesque in space,
So famous in the anglers' art, In fancy I may pace thy shores,
And treasure thy rare scenes in heart ; I picture thee with all thy isles,
Fair inlets crown'd with foliage screen. Their borders fring'd with silvery sand,
Embroider'd with the grasses green ;
Where dense groves droop their tresses o'er,
To dip them in the crystal wave, Where water lilies ope their cups,
And the cardinal red flowerets lave. There song birds build their airy nests
On chestnut branch and alder bush, Saluting with melodious hymns
The blushing dawns, the twilight hush, Till sweeter echoings thrill the air,
Entrancing all who listen there. Here, often in the vanished years,
The brilliant Herbert lov'd to roam ; Lover of nature, here he sought
Communion with her in her home ; Here lov'd with poet's eye to trace The
natural beauties of the place ;
Here lov'd   in these dense groves to stand,
And list the winds their sighs prolong Thro' the tall pines that shade the land ;
Soft winds, sweet as melodious song Hymn'd by cathedral's tuneful choir,

Swelling their music thro' the shades, Charming the woodlands with their lyre.
Thrilling the foliage in the glades, Soft-mingled with all sweet sounds heard, The lapse of brook, the song of bird.

O'er thy calm face, O Greenwood Lake, How beauteous the mornings break! How fair the twilight shadows sail O'er woods and waters of the vale ! The anglers, freed from toil and care, From crash of city thoroughfare, From fret and fume of square and pier, Fainting in breezeless atmosphere. Delighted, gleeful, hither come. As children seek parental home And here, forgetful of the past, Elate with hope, their tackle cast.

Years since, dear Herbert's ardent friends

Hop'd here a noble shaft to place, Bearing the name of him who lov'd To wander over Greenwood space. And consecrate with loving rite.

With song that thrill'd and speech that prais'd So one poor bard wrought native ode.

But yet, alas! no shaft was rais'd.

MOUNT TAHAWAS.

Toiling, we reach'd a bare, gigantic cone. The lofty summit of Tahawas Mount: How grand the view spread limitless!

There far-up skies we reach'd the utmost height, The loftiest region in the Empire State, The centre of a chaos of great cliffs. How diverse from the mountain range of Alps! Here rose no shining glaciers or snowy peaks, But all was gray or green to farthest view. It seems as if the Almighty had here set The vast earth rolling in tempestuous seas, And then in 'midst of its convulsive flow, Had bid the billows here congealing cease ; There they remain just as He froze the rocks, So grand and gloomy, in majestic height!

Here swept long swells, and there were bursting
waves,
There, too, the deep and cavernous black gulfs.

Far, far away, storm was raging fierce,

While massive clouds o'er Vermont's distant hills Stood motionless, as balanced in the skies;

Those far-off storms spread 'gainst the mountain
range.

With nought but savage scenery between! How grand, mysterious, awful did it seem ! Mount Golden with its precipices steep ;

                Mount McIntyre with black and barren head,
                  White Face with bright spot gleaming on its face.

And countless other summits pierced the air: Then, too, thick forests, boundless in extent, Green slopes and ridges, interspersed with lakes. Form'd wilderness, seamed here and there by
streams
Whose course was seen thro' gaps of lofty trees: Yes, there was beauty, grandeur in the scene! Lake Champlain, with its islands stretched afar, And the Green Mountains tower'd along the east. Far up the north gleam'd out Saranac Lakes, And nearer lakes in quiet beauty shone ;

Great lakes—some dark with girdling mounts. And others flashing out in landscape wide. Like smiles relieving the vast solitude!

It seemed as if we saw sublimity and strength : Vagueness and terror are embodied here! As if God wrought extremest power here. A mighty symbol of omnipotence !

And man is nothing here, a thing of nought !

THE SUMMER EXODUS.

Thrice happy, they, the darling sons of wealth To whom the boon is given to escape The city's granite walks, and roam afar.

Our favorite journals, with their welcome sheet, Point out the regions whither they may speed ; Tell them of happiest places of resort,

Where pallid cheek and broken health may seek New life, fresh vigor. and the glow of health :

Tell them where breezes blow, and woodlands green,

Bend their thick branches in refreshing shade ; Woods that are vocal with their fluttering leaves, Woods so melodious with the songs of birds ;

Great woods, like vast cathedrals, in whose domes And columned chapels, scarce a sunbeam falls : Secluded lanes where 'drooping willows grow, Where winding rills of ice-cold waters run,

And murmuring tell where lurk the springing trout ;

Tell them of fair resorts by Hudson's banks. Of Long Branch. Newport, Narragansett Pier. Of Martha's Vineyard and the Isle of Shoals.

Of Greenwood Lake, of the blue Lake of Schroon. Of the Green Mountains and of Lake Champlain, Of Saratoga's grand, palatial halls,

Of Old Point Comfort and the Chesapeake. Cape Ann and all its rocky solitudes;

The piny woods and rugged shores of Maine, The Lake George region and the Shawangunk. The Adirondack chain, the Catskill peaks,

The bowery shores of Jersey; sandy dunes That fringe Long Island's far extended beach, So far outspread. where league-long billows roll; Peconic Bay, and lovely Shelter Isle :

And countless other Eden-like resorts,

So rich with all their woods and waves and winds.

FORESTS AND STREAMS.

We sing of the forests, lonely and dim,

In whose intricate depths no sunbeam may gleam; The wild Adirondacks. the woodlands of Maine, Whose glooms are sublime, whose grandeur supreme!

For ages they stretch'd in boundless expanse,

For ages they cast their foliage to earth ;

They bloom'd in the Spring. in the Summers ma-
tured.

In the glory of Autumn their banners wav'd forth,

The scarlet of maple, the oak's ruddy gold, The yellow of beech, the elm's tender dyes, Here close interwove their rainbow-like hues, Receiving all tints that illumine the skies.

But, ah! there were glooms in their umbrage profound ;

Where the great solemn hemlocks their canopies wove,

Where the pines and the spruces towered in air,

And spread o'er the hills a primeval grove.

In secluded, dim haunts the wild creatures rov'd: The gaunt, grizzly bears in caverns would hide, The moose and the caribou gather'd in herds,

And the deer lept the rocks with marvelous
stride.

No pale-face hunters molested the game.

No echoes of rifles alarmed the red deer ; The Indian alone would ravage the wilds, Assailing with primitive arrow and spear.

But, ah, the wide streams, majestic and grand! No verse of the poet may sketch *ye* aright ; No brush of the artist, with palette and paint,

May depict on the canvas your loveliness bright! Methinks in a fanciful mood I may stand

By the shore of some stream of ample expanse. And enchanted gaze on the rippling tides,

The blue billows leaping in frolic dance. In restless tumult, in slumberous rest,

There's ever for me a supreme delight ;

For the woods and waters of Nature's realm Are glorified ever with fadeless light.

Milton Keynes UK
Ingram Content Group UK Ltd.
UKHW050710310324
440241UK00009BA/372